MODERN ART

Konecky & Konecky
72 Ayers Point Rd.
Old Saybrook, CT 06475

First published in 2005

05 07 09 08 06

1 3 5 7 9 8 6 4 2

Created and produced by **FLAME TREE PUBLISHING**,
Crabtree Hall, Crabtree Lane, Fulham, London SW6 6TY

ISBN: 1-56852-556-7

Printed in China

Publisher and Creative Director: Nick Wells
Development and Picture Research: Melinda Révész
Project Editor: Polly Willis
Editor: Sarah Goulding
Designer: Colin Rudderham
Production: Chris Herbert, Claire Walker

Special thanks to: Geoffrey Meadon, Sara Robson, Sarah Elliot and Helen Tovey

MODERN ART

Author: Michael Kerrigan   Foreword: Michael Robinson

Franz Kline, *Provincetown II*

KONECKY&KONECKY

Joan Miró, *Mythologization of Landscape (Dialogue of Insects)*

Contents

Andy Warhol, *Campbell's Soup*; Juan Gris, *Breakfast*; Georg Baselitz, *Studio Corner*

George Luks, *Hester Street*; Edward Hopper, *Chop Suey*; Helen Frankenthaler, *The Bay*

August Macke, *Woman in a Green Jacket*; Paul Klee, *The Lamb*; Franz Marc, *Springende Pferd*

Luigi Russolo, *Music*; Theo van Doesburg, *Contra-Composition of Dissonances XVI*; László Moholy-Nagy, *Architektur I*

Henri Gaudier-Brzeska, *Mermaid*; William Tucker, *Thebes*; Umberto Boccioni, *Unique Forms of Continuity in Space*

How To Use This Book

The reader is encouraged to use this book in a variety of ways, each of which caters for a range of interests, knowledge and uses.

- The book is organized into five sections: **Still Life**; **Landscape & Cityscape**; **Portrait**; **Abstract, Colour & Form**; and **Sculpture & 3D**. The text in all these sections provides the reader with a brief background to the work, and gives greater insight into how and why it was created.
- **Still Life** introduces the hugely varied genre that is modern art, focusing particularly on the way still life paintings have been interpreted in the modern era.
- **Landscape & Cityscape** takes a look at the many and varied depictions of environment and the techniques used, from traditional oil paintings to lithographs and collage.
- **Portrait** shows us how this genre has been revitalized, with weird and wonderful elongated and representational figures and more straightforward oil on canvas portraits.
- **Abstract, Colour & Form** includes works in a huge variety of sub-genres, from Futurism and Abstract Expressionism to Constructivism, Neo Expressionism and Pop Art.
- **Sculpture & 3D** showcases stunning sculptures and objects in a huge range of media, including bronze, wood, stone, brick, marble and even flourescent tubes.

2. Name of artist by surname,
then forename

1. Title of work

3. Date of painting (if known)

12. Picture credit

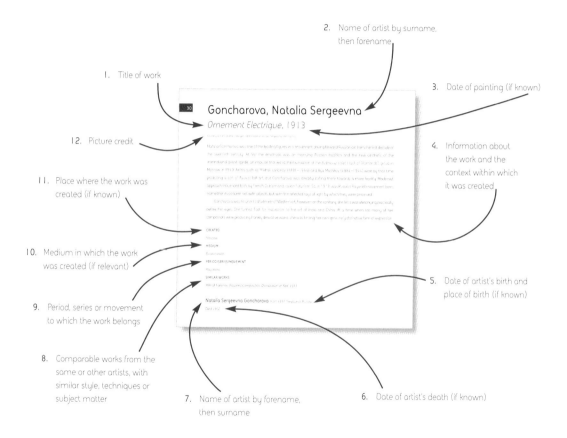

4. Information about
the work and the
context within which
it was created

11. Place where the work was
created (if known)

10. Medium in which the work
was created (if relevant)

5. Date of artist's birth and
place of birth (if known)

9. Period, series or movement
to which the work belongs

8. Comparable works from the
same or other artists, with
similar style, techniques or
subject matter

7. Name of artist by forename,
then surname

6. Date of artist's death (if known)

Foreword

Since you have picked up this book, you obviously have an interest in, or at the very least are curious to know more about, modern art. That's fine. However, it must be remembered that no book on modern art can claim to be a 'definitive guide', since art historians can't even agree on who was the first 'modern' artist. For some it was Edouard Manet who proffered his modernist credentials, 'by the frankness with which he declared the surfaces on which they were painted.' For others it was Pablo Picasso and his 'laboratory of (Cubist) art'. This academic discourse need not concern us here, but the general consensus is that a history of modern art equates to a history of the twentieth century.

At the beginning of the century, an attempt was made to synthesize all the elements of artistic progress in the late nineteenth century into an art that was specifically for the new epoch. It had to be progressive, notwithstanding the necessary homage and use of the basic artistic precepts of the previous epoch, namely painting and sculpture. This 'new' art was partially a response to Friedrich Nietzsche, whose writings had a particular currency at this time, calling for an art that sought to resolve the dichotomy of the Apollonian and Dionysian forces within an artist. Nietzsche saw art as a positive creative force in an otherwise nihilistic world, and artists as diverse as Picasso and members of the Brücke group were inspired by his writings.

However challenging Cubism and Fauvism were to representation and academic standards, the work executed in the first decade-and-a-half of the twentieth century was still based on the painting and sculpture traditions of Western art. The Great War changed all that, with the bourgeoisie held to be responsible for the carnage; art was seen as a symptom of, and contribution to, their decadence. Dada was born, and is still used today in its various guises, to critique politics, politicians, the bourgeoisie and artists who are perceived as conforming to bourgeois standards. Dada was, and still is, 'anti-art' designed to shock, anger and unsettle conventions. More importantly it was, and is, not meant to be logical, since logic was a trait of the bourgeoisie.

In the inter-war period, attempts were made to structure the various artistic movements or 'isms' into a chronology, adding kudos to the opening of the world's first museum of modern art in New York. The Museum of Modern Art succeeded in defining the modernist canon, determining who was and who was not within it.

The museum, financed by wealthy trustees such as the Rockefellers, had an exhibition policy determined by economic and political considerations, rather than artistic ideologies. The elevation of modern art to canonical status as part of a so-called 'high culture' rather missed the point since its whole *raison d'être* was to challenge the status quo both politically and artistically.

These ideas of a challenging art were resumed in the aftermath of the Second World War. Many European artists had made the east coast of America their home during the conflict, resulting in the birth of the so-called 'New York School'. The resultant Abstract Expressionism and its consequential 'end of painting' paved the way for new forms of art that challenged the status of art and artists, its function within society and the mediums that could be used to express such challenges. Many of the ideas were Dadaist-inspired anti-art that used new technologies to achieve the same end. Artists such as Andy Warhol questioned the validity of art's 'aura' in the wake of infinite reproducibility of images by ruthlessly exploiting mass media. Many artists staged 'performances' to express political ideologies such as Marxism and feminism, while others explored new mediums such as those used in 'land art'.

The creation of art has always been for an audience, requiring the viewer to participate at some level. Up until the twentieth century, the viewing effort was passive, requiring minimal effort since the artist had, invariably, created the anecdote within an illusionary picture space or on a plinth. The twentieth century radically altered that relationship, with the viewer required to take a more active role, sometimes as a participant in the work itself, in unpicking the meanings, motivations and agenda of the artist or artists.

Understanding modern art, if indeed it can or is meant to 'understood', is not just about reading its history or precedents. It is about an engagement with its ethos, a continuous metaphysical reinterpretation of an ever-changing world. As the artist Georges Braque said, 'Art is meant to disturb, science reassures.' Hopefully *Modern Art* will disturb you.

Michael Robinson, *2005*

Introduction

'The Twentieth Century – what intensity, what activity, what restless, nervous energy! Has there in six centuries been better art...?' Brave words; reckless ones indeed, and yet the sheer insouciance with which Arshile Gorky sweeps aside the likes of Michelangelo and Titian gives a hint as to why what he says is so very nearly true. Boldness and self-confidence were key to the artistic revolutions of the early twentieth century; art had never before been so sure that it could achieve anything it set out to, and that it really mattered. The colourful abandon of the Fauvists; the staggering boldness of Cubism; the epoch-making absurdity of Dada; the simplicity of *De Stijl* – developments like this were born of a deep conviction that it was up to art to define humanity's relation to its world. And define it to a considerable extent it did, not just through the works of such acknowledged modern titans as Matisse, Picasso, Kandinksy and Mondrian, but through the contributions of many more in what was by any historic standards a golden age of art. Their impact on society extended far beyond the avowedly politicized efforts of the Futurists, Soviet Constructivists and Social Realists: Modernism redefined what it was for the individual to perceive, to think, to be.

Modernism is a general term used to cover a multiplicity of movements seen in retrospect as working towards comparable ends. Yet words like 'movement' and 'school' themselves often encompass a great deal more variety than may at first appear. Helpful labels in principle, they may actually obscure more than they illuminate, if too rigidly and unquestioningly relied on. Schools such as Cubism, Futurism and Surrealism, for instance, were all working to definite and explicitly theorized artistic agendas; others such as the *École de Paris* ('School of Paris') are little more than catch-all categories. Even well-defined schools have their doctrinaire loyalists, their pragmatists and their incorrigible rebels, and by no means all movements are necessarily so well defined. Orphism had its origins within Cubism, for example, and only gradually parted company; its co-founder Sonia Delaunay in many ways kept faith with the Fauvism in which she had begun. 'Orphism', 'Cubism', 'Fauvism': all three are useful terms, since some sort of nomenclature is needed to make sense of those extraordinary times. Yet all three overlapped as ideas and individuals flowed back and forth between them: to regard them as having clear-cut demarcations may be misleading. Then there are the regional variations and also clear similarities, for example, between Italian Futurism, English Vorticism and Russian Rayonism, and not only in artistic form but in more general preoccupations. Ideologically, however, leading Futurists and Vorticists were hellbent on a course that would bring them into Fascism, while the Rayonists would soon be eager participants in the Russian Revolution.

One common, underlying theme we can perhaps identify in the art of the early twentieth century is a general tendency towards abstraction. It is worth reminding ourselves that this was genuinely new: where is the abstract art of the Renaissance, the Baroque? Even Turner and the Impressionists had been striving for higher forms of representation. The rise of abstraction in the twentieth century can be insisted upon too firmly; in 1936, Alfred H. Barr Jr, founding director of New York's Museum of Modern Art, produced his now-notorious flow chart of artistic influences since the 1890s. It clearly demonstrated, to his satisfaction at least, the 'inevitability' of the trend. By the 1940s, it suggested, there would really be no artistic option: you would be able to choose between geometrical or non-geometrical abstract art.

Things did not turn out quite that way, of course, and today Barr's diagram seems ridiculously reductive (although it serves as a handy *aide-mémoire* to the different movements of the early 1900s). It clearly shows the systematizing tendencies of the time, however, and how firmly rooted was the idea of history as being pre-determined 'progress', and not just in Marxist-influenced European thought. Barr obviously had a point, moreover. By the time he was making his prophecy, America's Regionalists and Social Realists seemed like throwbacks, whatever their inherent qualities. The apparently eternal truths of representational art had been breaking down since the 1890s: what Fauvism had done for colour, Cubism had gone on to do for outline, and Dada and Surrealism for the very idea of order. Even where the notion of art as representation endured, what this meant had often been so radically reinterpreted as to be unrecognizable by the conventions of before. Mondrian would, for example, set down to paint, not a tree, as an earlier landscape painter might have done, but what he saw as the spiritual 'truth' of a tree. It was representational art, then, but not as we might understand it. Kokoschka's 'psychological portraits' aimed to capture not the physical appearance of their subjects but the often tormented 'soul' within. The first 'true' abstracts – avowedly unrepresentational works – had been painted quite some time before: Kandinsky holds this title, for his 'non-objective' works of 1913. Of more significance, however, is the extent to which the 'abstract spirit' was abroad in art – Barr's claims were not as outrageous as they may seem.

As the middle of the twentieth century approached, then, art seemed to have its future all mapped out, but a series of shocks would derail the smooth progression. One was the great cataclysm of the Second World War. The First World War, in human terms a greater calamity for Europe, had at least actually lent impetus to art. Jean Arp was to describe how Dada, born in Zurich in 1915, was horrified by the 'slaughterhouses of the world war'. Artists looked to find an art

You can't drag your money into the grave with you

Barbara Kruger, *Untitled (You can't drag your money into the grave with you)*. Courtesy of Hamburg Kunsthalle, Hamburg, Germany/www.bridgeman.co.uk/© Barbara Kruger

that would 'save mankind from the furious folly of these times'. In precipitating the events of the Russian Revolution of 1917, the war, for a time at least, seemed to have opened up a new era of optimism and freedom. The Second World War was different: *blitzkrieg* and carpet bombing, 'total war', had brought the conflict home to Paris, London, Berlin and Dresden – and then, of course, there had been the 'Final Solution' of the Nazis. Theodor Adorno famously wondered whether it wasn't 'barbaric' to write poetry after Auschwitz, and modern art would suffer a similar loss of nerve. The Abstract Expressionism of the 1950s has a yearning, questing character very different from the upbeat intrepidness that went before.

More shocks were in store: a rapidly advancing technology and burgeoning mass media soon threatened to render the artist as an individual genius redundant. Images could be mass-produced to order (and to standards that mocked the representational efforts of traditional art). Would art as such be redundant? Would the individual sculptor or painter have a role beyond the creation of civic statues or portraits for the boardroom? The Pop Artists of the 1960s joined a mass culture they clearly couldn't beat, but how long would it be before even this contribution was marginalized? To begin with, at least, the imprimatur of 'high art' on everything from soup tins to the Beatles was gratefully received, but soon the mass culture would feel no need of such endorsement. All that the artist had to offer, it sometimes seemed, was his or her authenticating signature and the fact that what he or she created was unique. This was no small consideration, of course: a world in which imagery was being industrially produced naturally set a premium on what was original and what was, as it were, 'handcrafted'. The fine-art market boomed, fortunes were made, and from a certain standpoint artists had never had it so good. However, was this really a vocation or just a living?

Gabriele Munter, *Village Street in Winter*. Courtesy of The Art Archive/Städtische Galerie im Lenbachhaus Munich/Dagli Orti/© Estate of Gabriele Munter

Meanwhile, developments in linguistics and philosophy were beginning to 'deconstruct' the central assumptions of Modernism. Was there any such thing as transcendent 'truth' or essential 'being'? Were our perceptions, our feelings, our very selves, anything more than 'constructs' of the words we used to describe and express them? Were we just the creations of our culture, the articulations of our place and time? 'All that is solid melts into air', Marx had said of the intellectual impact of industrialism; something of the same now happened as the developed world entered the 'information age'. Yet the dissolution of old certainties, disorientating as it was, would by no means be an entirely negative experience as things turned out. Dwarfing our information-crunching capacities, computers threatened our uniqueness (the question of whether they could really *think* was being asked seriously), but they would also be a profoundly liberating force. Even as our sense of 'deep' selfhood was being undermined, a lighter version was being reasserted and a new spirit of playful 'Postmodernism' was unleashed. We might have no 'essence' any more,

René Magritte, *Time Transfixed*, Courtesy of Art Institute of Chicago, IL, USA/www.bridgeman.co.uk/© ADAGP, Paris & DACS, London 2005

but we could have as many online identities as we liked. We might have lost our faith in fine art's redemptive powers, but we could cut and paste the imagery of the past to our heart's content. Quotation, allusion and parody were the substance of an art that no longer believed in substance. It was a bewildering world; many felt unmoored and intellectually adrift. Still, as the twentieth century drew to its close, there was a real sense of expectation: what would art do next? The possibilities were endless.

Modern Art

Still Life

Matisse, Henri
Still Life with 'La Danse', 1909

'What I am after, above all, is expression,' wrote Henri Matisse in 1908, and he set out to achieve this chiefly through his use of colour. But making a living was important too, as we see in the extraordinary piece of product placement which sees *La Danse*, an earlier work by Matisse, appearing, as though incidentally, in the background of his scene. The self-advertisement is a reminder of how large the market loomed in the painter's life in an art world in which private collectors, rather than ecclesiastical or aristocratic patrons, had come to dominate. Eager to possess the latest thing, and where possible to upstage one another with the originality and daring of the works they bought, such collectors had a significant (if unquantifiable) influence on the development of twentieth-century art.

Matisse was famously a leading light in the circle of Parisian painters known as *les fauves* ('wild beasts'), but the label obscures as much as it illuminates. The wildness certainly comes across here in a palette that assaults the visual sense, and in the paradox of a 'still life' whose surging energy makes it seem anything but still.

CREATED

Paris

MEDIUM

Oil on canvas

PERIOD/SERIES/MOVEMENT

Fauvism

SIMILAR WORKS

Raoul Dufy, *Still Life with Bananas*, c. 1909

Henri Matisse *Born* 1869 Picardy, France

Died 1954

de Vlaminck, Maurice

Nature Morte Fauve ('Fauve Still Life'), 1906

'I never ask a friend how he makes love to his wife in order to love mine, nor what woman I ought to love, and I never worry about how women were loved in 1802.' These defiant words were written in 1923, in what purported to be a letter to a friend, but was really Maurice de Vlaminck's artistic manifesto. 'I have no one but myself to please,' it continued, concluding in ringing if decidedly eccentric terms, 'I never go to funerals, I do not dance on the 14th of July, I do not play the horses or demonstrate in the streets. I adore children.'

Today, any self-respecting artist is expected to be outrageous, off the wall, and this is an assumption for which the Fauves must take a great deal of credit for establishing. Maurice de Vlaminck was an outsider both in bourgeois and bohemian terms, having come to art after a successful career as a professional racing cyclist. He felt a natural affinity with Fauvism and above all he loved colour — bold, unmixed and unmoderated, often squeezing it straight on to the canvas from the tube.

CREATED

Paris

MEDIUM

Oil on canvas

PERIOD/SERIES/MOVEMENT

Fauvism

SIMILAR WORKS

André Derain, *The Table*, 1906

Othon Friesz, *Still Life with Anemones*, c. 1910

Maurice de Vlaminck *Born* Paris 1876

Died 1958

Gris, Juan
Breakfast, 1915

Paradoxical, even perverse in its workings, Cubism did more than any other movement to free modern painting from the mimetic responsibilities of old. It defied the two-dimensionality of the canvas, it dismantled every scene into its component planes, and it made items square so that they could be exhibited 'in the round'.

The vogue for Cubism swept Paris in the decade before the First World War. For its greatest practitioners, though, it was far more than a fashion. Gertrude Stein, the émigrée American writer and champion of all things avant-garde, noted that to Juan Gris in particular Cubism was 'a religion'. She meant in part that Gris was more at pains than most to follow through a theory of aesthetics in his work, and to systematize what for others might be no more than an ad hoc device or posture. 'Truth is beyond any realism,' he said, 'and the appearance of things should not be confused with their essence.' Stein also put a finger on something clearly evidenced in this remarkably atmospheric still life: the profound spirituality underlying what might seem no more than a geometrical game.

CREATED

Paris

MEDIUM

Oil on canvas

PERIOD/SERIES/MOVEMENT

Cubism

SIMILAR WORKS

Pablo Picasso, *Still Life with Chair-Caning*, 1912

Juan Gris *Born* 1887 Madrid, Spain

Died 1927

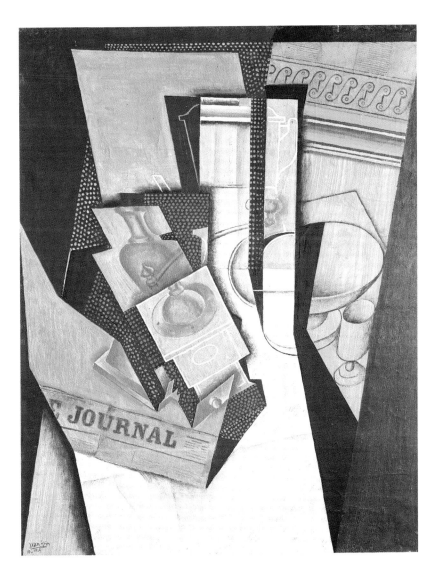

Carrà, Carlo

Interventionist Manifesto, 1914

As first propounded by the writer Tommaso Marinetti in 1909, Futurism embraced all that was brash and powerful, even violent. 'We will glorify war – the only true hygiene of the world ... We will destroy museums and libraries, and fight against moralism, feminism and all utilitarian cowardice.' Two global conflicts and several genocides later, such sentiments have a ring of boyish bravado, too silly even to be convincingly sinister.

But, for all its absurd posturings, Marinetti's *Futurist Manifesto* does deserve the credit for jump-starting the 'roaring automobile' of Futurism, although it would be artists, not writers, who actually got it going. In between the sound and the fury, Marinetti was putting forward more interesting ideas. Carlo Carrà is clearly responding here to his mentor's call for an art that 'no longer satisfied with form and colour' as previously understood, but sought to catch 'the dynamic sensation itself'. He clearly found the anarchically festive streak in Marinetti's philosophy more appealing than the taste for sheer destruction. His aim, he said, was to evoke 'all the colours of speed, of joy, of carousings and fantastic carnivals'.

CREATED

Milan

PERIOD/SERIES/MOVEMENT

Futurism

SIMILAR WORKS

Umberto Boccioni, *Materia*, 1912

Giacomo Balla, *Study of Materiality of Lights and Speed*, 1913

Carlo Carrà *Born* 1881 Piedmont, Italy

Died 1966

Goncharova, Natalia Sergeevna
Ornement Electrique, 1913

Courtesy of CKS Christie's Images Ltd/© Estate of Natalia Sergeevna Goncharova

Natalia Goncharova was one of the leading figures in a movement driving forward Russian art from the first decade of the twentieth century. At first the emphasis was on marrying Russian tradition and the new aesthetic of the international avant-garde, an impulse that led to the foundation of the *Bubnovyi Valet* ('Jack of Diamonds') group in Moscow in 1910. Artists such as Mikhail Larionov (1881–1964) and Ilya Mashkov (1881–1944) were by that time producing a sort of Fauvist folk art, but Goncharova was already pulling them towards a more frankly Modernist approach influenced both by French Cubism and Italian Futurism. So, in 1913, was Russia's Rayonist movement born, named for its concern not with objects, but with the reflected rays of light by which they were perceived.

Goncharova was no uncritical admirer of Western art, however; on the contrary, she felt it was atrophying practically before her eyes. She turned East for inspiration, to the art of India and China. At a time when too many of her compatriots were producing frankly derivative works, she was finding her own genuinely distinctive form of expression.

CREATED

Moscow

MEDIUM

Oil on canvas

PERIOD/SERIES/MOVEMENT

Rayonism

SIMILAR WORKS

Mikhail Larionov, *Rayonist Composition: Domination of Red*, 1911

Natalia Sergeevna Goncharova *Born* 1881 Negayevo, Russia

Died 1962

Stepanova, Varvara Fedorovna

Collage, c. 1919

Creative artists have always resisted, and often resented, the view that their work should offer a refuge from real life, and this was never more so than in times of political ferment and social transformation. It is hardly surprising, then, that Russian artists of the early twentieth century should have found inspiration in the revolutionary struggle.

Launched by Vladimir Tatlin (1885–1953) in 1914, Constructivism was clearly influenced by the works of Pablo Picasso, who at that time was experimentally incorporating bits of cardboard, string and other odd items semi-sculpturally into his painted works. In the Soviet context, however, such techniques acquired an almost sacral significance, given the reverence accorded to the labour of the workers in building the new society. Many Constructivists, including Tatlin himself, found abstract sculptures assembled from wood, steel and other building materials to offer the closest possible analogy between art and industrial work. Others, like Stepanova and her husband Alexander Rodchenko (1891–1956), pursued a more painterly path to the same end. This work subjects the landscape scene of artistic convention and the land-holding system of Russian tradition to the straight edges and angular forms of the new industrialism.

CREATED

Moscow

MEDIUM

Collage on paper

PERIOD/SERIES/MOVEMENT

Constructivism

Varvara Fedorovna Stepanova *Born* 1894 Kovno, Lithuania .

Died Moscow, 1958

Schwitters, Kurt

Collage M2 439, 1922

The word 'Dada' took its name from a French colloquialism for 'hobbyhorse' and was found at random, the story goes, in a rifle through the dictionary. True or not, this account is appropriate given the movement's eager embracing of anarchic chance and serendipity in reaction to what its founders saw as the hidebound and highly restrictive traditions of bourgeois culture. The first centre of Dada was in Zurich, Switzerland, where a group grew up around the central figures of Jean Arp (1886–1966) and Hans Richter (1888–1976); the movement found a lively spokesman in the Romanian poet Tristan Tzara. Other like-minded cliques were soon forming as far afield as New York, Berlin and even Hanover, where Kurt Schwitters had built his own one-man movement.

Schwitters coined his own meaningless word, 'Merz', to describe his new nonsensical aesthetic, which involved placing odds and ends of 'found' rubbish randomly together to create collages. 'Merz', he said, 'means freedom from all fetters, for the sake of artistic creation. Freedom is not lack of restraint, but the product of strict artistic discipline'.

CREATED

Hanover

MEDIUM

Collage on paper

PERIOD/SERIES/MOVEMENT

Dada (Merz)

SIMILAR WORKS

Jean Arp, *Collage Created by the Laws of Chance*, 1916–17

Kurt Schwitters *Born* 1887 Hanover, Germany

Died 1948

Schamberg, Morton

God, 1917

The American artist's own sculpture becomes a still-life picture in this toned gelatin silver photograph: a piece of rusty piping on a pedestal. Did Schamberg set out to outrage respectable religious sensibilities when he called this assemblage of scrap metal 'God', or was he satirizing his society's materialism and idolization of technology?

Deliberate blasphemy is by no means entirely out of the question; for all its playfulness, Dada had an aggressive and iconoclastic streak. Yet Schamberg was just as likely to have been motivated by the way the image summed up for him creativity founded in the recontextualization of objects through improbable juxtapositions. Schamberg's technique comes close to the use of what Marcel Duchamp (1887–1968) called 'readymades': manufactured objects re-presented as works of art. Their impact lay not in careful composition or skilful execution, but in the ability of the artist and the viewer to perceive new possibilities in the commonplace. As such, the new aesthetic can be seen as a descendant (albeit a distant one) of Romanticism, but there is no doubting the shock that such innovations gave rise to in their day.

CREATED

Philadelphia

MEDIUM

Toned gelatin silver photograph

PERIOD/SERIES/MOVEMENT

Dada

SIMILAR WORKS

Marcel Duchamp, *Bicycle Wheel*, 1913

Morton Schamberg *Born* 1881, Philadelphia, USA

Died 1918

Le Corbusier
(Jeanneret, Charles Edouard)
Still Life With Many Eyes, 1923

No single individual did more to shape the physical fabric of twentieth-century society than 'Le Corbusier', prophet of a high-tech future and proponent of the 'International Style' in architecture. Applying his enthusiasm for all things industrial to the routine rhythms of everyday existence, he famously insisted that the house should be a 'machine for living'; he attacked the taste for ornament, instead elevating all that was sparse and functional. His theories inspired hundreds of shapely structures in steel, concrete and glass. But before he made the architectural interventions for which he would become famous, Jeanneret was making a modest but influential impact as a painter. In 1918, with his friend, the French painter Amédée Ozenfant (1886–1966), he launched a new movement that he called 'Purism'. Ornamentation was out, and the same fascination with mechanization was evident. 'The picture is a machine for the transmission of sentiments,' they asserted.

CREATED

Paris

MEDIUM

Oil on canvas

PERIOD/SERIES/MOVEMENT

Purism

SIMILAR WORKS

Amédée Ozenfant, *Still Life: Dishes*, 1920

Charles Edouard Jeanneret *Born* 1887 Switzerland

Died 1965

Ozenfant, Amédée

The White Pitcher, 1925

The aggressive rhetoric of Purists Jeanneret and Ozenfant should not be taken too simply at face value: a conservative impulse informed their desire for radical change. They revered the machine for the intricate logic and neatness of design they saw embodied in its workings, not for the noise, fumes and destructive power that so thrilled the Futurists.

Order, grace and chastity are the key to this composition – the predominant values of Purism were very much those of Classicism. Jeanneret and Ozenfant were working in reaction to what they saw as the degeneration of Cubism into something approaching merely ornamental clutter. The original aims of the Cubists were respected: the Purists, too, tried to reveal space in plane surfaces, but they were eager as well to celebrate the simplicity of forms. As an artistic movement Purism may have been swept away, with Ozenfant in particular, quite unjustly, all but forgotten now. However, the sensibility it established has persisted, extending far beyond the area of high art into every aspect of design, where we still take pleasure in the 'cool' qualities of uncrowded spaces and unfussy lines.

CREATED

Paris

MEDIUM

Oil on canvas

PERIOD/SERIES/MOVEMENT

Purism

SIMILAR WORKS

Charles Edouard Jeanneret, *Abstraction (Violins and Bottles)*, 1925

Amédée Ozenfant *Born* 1886 St Quentin, France

Died 1966

Bayer, Herbert

Sheet Music, 1921

Architect Walter Gropius (1883–1969) established the Bauhaus ('House for Building') in Weimar, Germany, in 1919. His aim was to bring artistic principles to bear on the design and construction of everything from buildings to lamps and to give the artist a real function in society. The emphasis was on 'applied' art, then, but 'pure' painting had its place: the Bauhaus' first director of art was Wassily Kandinsky (1866–1944), Bayer's master and later his teaching colleague at the Bauhaus.

Along with the great works of abstraction for which he is now famous, Kandinsky had produced a profoundly influential book, *Concerning the Spiritual in Modern Art* (1911). It proposed a mystic vision of art, bringing music and painting together to promote a 'spiritual change' in those who experienced it, touching them at a level beyond that of any superficial 'beauty'. Such an art already existed, Kandinsky suggested, in the 'atonal' music of Arnold Schoenburg; a comparable art would codify colours as 'vibrations of the soul'. Suggestions of such a mystic order (and allusions to musical instruments and notation) can clearly be seen in Bayer's composition.

CREATED

Weimar

MEDIUM

Watercolour and pencil on paper

PERIOD/SERIES/MOVEMENT

Bauhaus

SIMILAR WORKS

Paul Klee, *Tänzerpaar*, 1923

Herbert Bayer *Born* 1900 Haag, Austria

Died 1985

Soutine, Chaïm

Le Poulet Plumé , 1925

The so-called *École de Paris* ('School of Paris') was really no more than a loose community, its members sharing little more than a passion for art and an exile's status in the Paris of the interwar period. Subgroups inevitably formed, none more interesting than that which was known as *Les Maudits* ('The Accursed'). Young artists are given to striking melodramatic postures, but this group did lead self-consciously wretched lives, 'cursed' by poverty, illness and their own out-of-control behaviour. The paintings of Maurice Utrillo (1883–1955) exude benignity and cheerfulness, and while those of the Bulgarian Jules Pascin (1885–1930) are admittedly stranger, it is only with Chaïm Soutine that a sense of malediction informs the work. Simply by being a painter, he had made himself a pariah in his native Lithuanian Jewish community: their orthodoxy deeply disapproved of the making of images. And such images! Soutine was fascinated by the dead and the disgusting: his own home was notoriously filthy and he toured abattoirs to study slaughtered flesh. Hence a still life like this one, its denuded carcasses grotesquely burlesquing the sleek game bird forms traditional to the genre.

CREATED

Paris

MEDIUM

Oil on canvas

PERIOD/SERIES/MOVEMENT

École de Paris/Expressionism

SIMILAR WORKS

Maurice Utrillo, *Flowers*

Chaïm Soutine *Born* 1893 Smilovichi, Lithuania

Died 1943

Agar, Eileen
Precious Stones, 1936

Courtesy of Leeds Museums and Galleries (City Art Gallery) UK/www.bridgeman.co.uk/© Estate of Eileen Agar

Eileen Agar stood out in the Paris of the 1930s, not so much because she was a female artist, but on account of being that still rarer creature, an English Surrealist. British writers and artists have often been uncomfortable with the Continental mania for movements and schools, their intellectual tradition favouring pragmatism over theoretical rigour. Characteristically, Agar herself, despite her position as Surrealism's main champion in the English-speaking world, steered clear of the furious pamphleteering of her contemporaries. To the followers of André Breton, Surrealism may have been dream-like but it was never vague; 'psychic automatism' was pursued as though it was a science. Surrealists found inspiration in the psychoanalytic insights of Sigmund Freud, but were at odds as to how they should be embodied in art. Eileen Agar was more concerned with creating artworks than with publishing manifestos, and her work can seem almost down-to-earth and common-sensical by Surrealist standards. This collage is quirky rather than weird: it is typical too in that, notwithstanding its rectangular shape, it is as much a three-dimensional 'object' as a painting in the usual sense.

CREATED

Paris

MEDIUM

Collage, mixed media

PERIOD/SERIES/MOVEMENT

Surrealism

SIMILAR WORKS

Joan Miró, *Peinture*, 1927

Eileen Agar *Born* 1899 Buenos Aires, Brazil

Died 1991

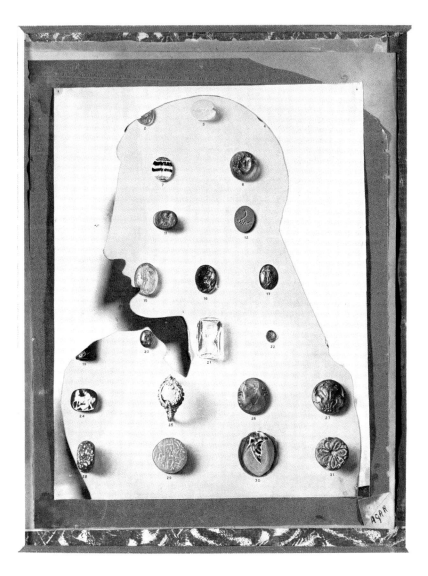

Magnelli, Alberto

Weighted Mass, 1958

Movements proliferated in twentieth-century painting, and most of them involved unfamiliar shapes and colours and distorted (or non-figurative) forms. The radicalism of 'Concrete Art' is easily underestimated. Unlike Abstract art, which begins with a motif from nature that is then abstracted by the artist, Concrete art has no motif: it is purely a product of the artist's mind. Not only did practitioners reject the idea that art had to 'stand for' anything, they also scorned the traditional task of representation and the more secondary significance of images, symbols and implied sentiments. 'We want,' declared Theo Van Doesburg, who launched the movement in 1930, 'to exclude lyricism, dramaticism, symbolism, etc, etc ... The picture has no other significance than "itself".' The work of art did not depict anything, therefore: it simply was. Because the whole muddle of meaning and emotion had been stripped away, what remained amounted to the distilled essence of artistic creation. It was inevitably an aesthetic of spareness: pictures and sculptures tended to take the form of simple planes and geometric forms, but the result is often, as here, artistic achievements of stunning beauty.

CREATED

Paris

MEDIUM

Oil on canvas

PERIOD/SERIES/MOVEMENT

Concrete Art

SIMILAR WORKS

Max Bill, *6-teillige Bewegung, 1: 2: 3* ('6 Parts in motion: 1, 2, 3'), *c.* 1944

Alberto Magnelli *Born* 1888, Italy, Florence

Died 1971

Magritte, René
Time Transfixed, 1938

'I decided to paint the image of a locomotive,' wrote René Magritte. 'In order for its mystery to be evoked, another *immediately* familiar image without mystery – the image of a dining room fireplace – was joined.' The presentation of ordinary items in extraordinary juxtaposition is crucial to Surrealist art, as it is to dreams. The Surrealists loved to quote a line from the nineteenth-century French poet Lautréamont: 'Beautiful as the chance encounter of a sewing machine and an umbrella on a dissecting table'. Such work also picks up on a principle already insisted on by those Dadaists who worked with 'found' objects and 'readymades'; namely that the creative vision can turn the mundane into great art. This principle was more gloriously attested in the ingenious yoking together of commonplace things than in the creation of new and intrinsically exotic forms. Belgian-born Magritte lived his own life in much the same spirit: originally a commercial designer, he maintained the daily routines of an office worker through his decades of artistic fame. He was down-to-earth in other ways too: like Salvador Dali (1904–89), he worked hard and meticulously for his extravagant effects.

CREATED

Brussels

MEDIUM

Oil on canvas

PERIOD/SERIES/MOVEMENT

Magic Realism/Surrealism

SIMILAR WORKS

Salvador Dali, *The Persistence of Memory*, 1931

René Magritte *Born* 1898 Lessines, Belgium

Died 1967

Roy, Pierre

Still Life With Shells, c. 1930

Magic casements, opening on the foam

Of perilous seas, in faery lands forlorn.

The sense of the infinite sea as a realm of fathomless mystery and unlimited possibility haunted many modern painters, just as it had done the poet Keats a century before.

The ocean recurs as a backdrop in works by the 'Magic Realists' of the 1930s and 1940s. Some works of Magritte, for example, have been given the 'Magic Realist' label, and the works of painters like Roy himself, his Belgian contemporary Paul Delvaux and American artists such as Peter Blume, Louis Guglielmi, Ivan Albright and George Tooker, started out from Magritte's technique of giving unexpected twists to realistically depicted scenes to create a mood of enchantment. Magic Realism dispensed with the pseudoscientific pretensions of Surrealism and its claims to be rigorously investigating the human psyche, hence its appeal to artists from a more pragmatic Anglo-Saxon tradition. Its real subject was the magic that was artistic representation. Here shore, sea and sky are seen as through the curtained stage of a theatre, a picture framed within the picture frame.

CREATED

Paris

PERIOD/SERIES/MOVEMENT

Magic Realism/Surrealism

SIMILAR WORKS

Peter Blume, *The Eternal City*, 1937

Pierre Roy *Born* 1880 Nantes, France 1880

Died 1950

Bratby, John
Still Life with Wardrobe, c. 1954

In the middle of the twentieth century, many painters in Continental Europe were turning towards an ideologically inspired concern with 'Social Realism', as unabashed in its representationalism as it was unsparing in its details. Italian painters such as Armando Pizzinato (b. 1910) and Renato Guttuso (1912–87), for example, made no secret of the fact that they saw their depictions of squalid interiors as a prompt to social and political change.

Coined by the critic David Sylvester in 1954, the title 'Kitchen Sink School' was bestowed on a group of British artists. Londoner John Bratby, as well as Sheffield-born Jack Smith (b. 1928) and Derrick Greaves (b. 1927), created deliberately drab, often dismal, domestic interiors and still-life scenes. Less explicitly political than their European contemporaries, their work struck a chord in its bleakness with the prevailing mood in post-war Britain. This was one of disillusionment and cynicism: victory had brought only austerity, it seemed – rationing was still in force, as were the class distinctions and moral prudery of old. The 'Kitchen Sink School' seemed to express the same outrage as that expressed in John Osborne's play *Look Back in Anger* (1956) and developed by a generation of 'Angry Young Men' thereafter.

CREATED

London

MEDIUM

Oil on board

PERIOD/SERIES/MOVEMENT

'Kitchen Sink' Realism

SIMILAR WORKS

Jack Smith, *Still Life with Bowl of Cherries*

John Bratby *Born* 1928, London, England

Died 1992

Johns, Jasper

Three Flags, 1958

In the 1950s, American Neo-Dadaists pioneered the trail that a decade later would lead to the 'Pop Art' of Andy Warhol (1928–62) and Roy Lichtenstein (b. 1923). The affection for American mass culture is already evident in their works. Jasper Johns (b. 1930) and Robert Rauschenberg (b. 1925) had worked together as window-dressers in New York department stores, so their feel for mass taste was no mere affectation. Despite this, their project was unabashedly highbrow; its aim to reveal overfamiliar objects in a new way, but there was nothing vulgarian about them – quite the contrary. Their embrace of what might seem banal sprang, as it had for their Dadaist predecessors, from a conviction that aesthetic value was not intrinsic to any object, but endowed by the artist in the actions of selection and setting forth for viewing.

Such purity of purpose may be appealing, but it is notoriously difficult to maintain, as the cultural context invariably intervenes. The problem is perfectly illustrated by Johns' depictions of the United States' flag: despite his protestations, the political climate of America during the Cold War years was such that it was inevitably received in a political spirit, whether of straightforward patriotism or ironic satire.

CREATED

New York

MEDIUM

Oil on canvas

PERIOD/SERIES/MOVEMENT

American Neo-Dada

SIMILAR WORKS

Robert Rauschenberg, *Bed*, 1955

Jasper Johns Born 1930 Augusta, GA, USA

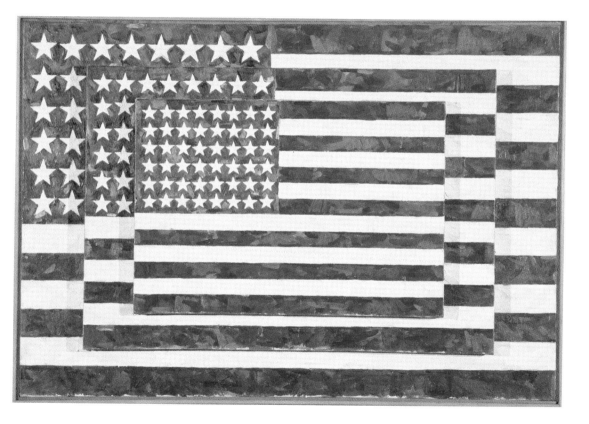

Rivers, Larry
Ford, 1961

Courtesy of Hamburg Kunsthalle, Hamburg, Germany/www.bridgeman.co.uk/© Larry Rivers/VAGA, New York/DACS, London 2005

No name was more closely associated with the values of mass production and the international mass-market in the twentieth century than that of the American auto-giant Ford. Here it inspires a painting that practically bursts with *joie de vivre*. Their ideas largely rooted in a Marxist model of history and cultural development, European artists viewed big business with suspicion. Americans were by and large more upbeat, their mood buoyed by a decade's post-war prosperity. They were fascinated, too, by the artistic implications of the endlessly repeated procedures involved in industrial manufacturing and by the infinite reproduction of images in advertising, both of which challenged the po-faced fetish for the unique that they saw in traditional art. Naïve as it may seem now, in an age of anti-globalization protests, American Neo-Dadaist artists saw signs of hope in the worldwide export of American popular culture. A shared pleasure in American media and consumer goods seemed set to unite the world in a brotherhood of man that could hardly have contrasted more starkly with the dour internationalism on offer from world Communism.

CREATED

New York

MEDIUM

Oil on canvas

PERIOD/SERIES/MOVEMENT

American Neo-Dada

SIMILAR WORKS

Claes Oldenberg, *7-Up*, 1961

Larry Rivers *Born* 1923 New York, USA

Died 2002

Caulfield, Patrick

Sweet Bowl, 1967

The term 'Pop Art' was first used in 1958, anticipating the 1960s revolution in pop music by some years. The phrase was coined by critic Lawrence Alloway: it neatly encapsulated the inspiration, sometimes, but by no means invariably, 'camp' and ironic, that was to be found in commercial art of every kind, from children's cartoons to advertising posters. As developed by friends of Alloway, such as Eduardo Paolozzi (1924–2005), Pop Art was not so very different from the American Neo-Dadaism of Jasper Johns (b. 1930) and Larry Rivers (b. 1923). What changed, in fact, was not so much the art itself as the cultural context. British pop music was taking the world by storm. By the mid-1960s, interest in the Beatles and other pop groups was clearly transcending their primary 'teen' market, and self-conscious sophisticates were taking an interest in their music. In response, performers moved on from the bouncy dance records and sentimental ballads that had made them famous to create self-consciously intellectual records. In music and art alike, pastiche was key: the means by which the clichés of mass culture were raised above the commonplace to the status of 'high' art.

CREATED

London

MEDIUM

Screen print

PERIOD/SERIES/MOVEMENT

Pop Art

SIMILAR WORKS

David Hockney, *Peter Getting Out of Nick's Pool*, 1966–67

Patrick Caulfield *Born* 1936 London, UK

Died 2002

Warhol, Andy

Campbell's Soup, 1968

This world-famous soup tin elbowed Marilyn Monroe into second place as the most immediately recognizable image of the Pop Art era. Warhol arguably did more than any other individual to create the widely held impression that modern art was a lot of nonsense, and few have done as much to keep art at the centre of the cultural stage. He dealt unashamedly in the ephemeral, said notoriously that everyone should be famous for 15 minutes, yet 40 years on, his fame seems set to be enduring. He was never simply a painter: his role was more that of entrepreneur or impresario. Founder of a pop group, the Velvet Underground, and presiding figure in a varied circle of creative painters and sculptors centred on his studio, 'The Factory', he became an unavoidable presence in American and international art of the 1960s.

Was Warhol a great artist, or an artist at all? He has little obviously in common with Leonardo da Vinci or even Pablo Picasso. However, banal as the images with which he works may be, he transmutes them into something altogether stranger and more startling, an artistic achievement by any definition.

CREATED

New York

MEDIUM

Screen print

PERIOD/SERIES/MOVEMENT

Pop Art

SIMILAR WORKS

James Rosenquist, *Firepole*, 1966–67

Andy Warhol (born Andrew Warhola) *Born* 1928 Pittsburgh, USA

Died 1987

Baselitz, Georg
Studio Corner, 1973

Courtesy of Hamburg Kunsthalle, Hamburg, Germany/www.bridgeman.co.uk/© George Baselitz

Raw, reckless in execution and often unsettlingly emotional in mood, Neo-Expressionism began in Germany just as the original Expressionism of the 1920s had done. Coined in conscious reaction to the term 'Impressionism', which saw art as a record of the world, with the creative mind as a kind of camera, Expressionism had been about the artist projecting his own feelings on to the world.

The feeling grew in the 1970s that the vogue for Pop Art, however apparently outrageous it was, was essentially just as 'passive' in the face of reality as Impressionism: Warhol's soup tins were as accepting of external appearances as Monet's water lilies had been. Georg Baselitz was so far from allowing his work to be dictated by such appearances that, from 1969, he started painting his figurative images upside down. The point, of course, was to prioritize the painting itself, its colours, lines and textures, over what it might be supposed to represent. *Studio Corner* features a female figure, nude. Her depiction is clearly anything but realistic, yet even so the picture simply pulsates with life.

CREATED

West Berlin

MEDIUM

Watercolour and coloured chalks

PERIOD/SERIES/MOVEMENT

Neo-Expressionism

SIMILAR WORKS

Anselm Kiefer, *The Book*, 1979–85

Georg Baselitz *Born Saxony, Germany, 1938*

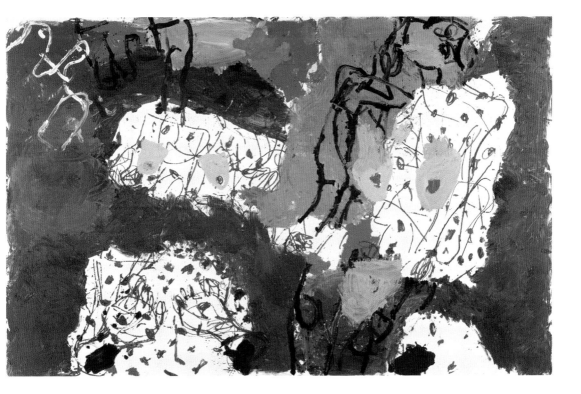

Kruger, Barbara

Untitled (You can't drag your money into the grave with you), 1990

Courtesy of Hamburg Kunsthalle, Hamburg, Germany/www.bridgeman.co.uk/© Barbara Kruger

'The only vindication of art is art,' wrote Joseph Kosuth in 1969: 'Art is the definition of art'. For a new generation, heirs to the revolutions that had already taken place in twentieth-century painting and sculpture, art's traditional duty of representation had come to seem meaningless, yet the sense of art's importance was if anything stronger than ever. Rather than depicting reality, art had become to them a critical commentary upon itself; works did not imitate nature, but reflected on the processes of art and its place in the wider culture. That meant a more critical engagement with the role of art in society, not just the joyous celebration of popular imagery *à la* Warhol. This piece, the pair of shoes indicating the space where a wealthy businessman might have been, questions the materialism of modern society. It makes ironic play of the conventions of commercial art: it could be seen as an anti-advertising advertising poster. But such ironies have often rebounded, the visual innovations of conceptual art being seized upon by an increasingly sophisticated advertising industry.

CREATED

New York

MEDIUM

Screen print on vinyl

PERIOD/SERIES/MOVEMENT

Appropriation Art/Postmodernism

SIMILAR WORKS

Martha Rosler, *Red Stripe Kitchen*, c. 1990

Barbara Kruger *Born* 1945 Newark, NJ, USA

Craig-Martin, Michael
... *and a cello*, 2002

A deceptive simplicity characterizes Michael Craig-Martin's work: 'I have tried to strip away everything inessential,' the Irish-born British artist says. His creations, he continues, seek 'to touch the line between art and the world, meaning and no meaning, feeling and no feeling ... Through extreme clarity and explicitness, I have tried to confirm mystery and depth'.

The screen print shown here is typical: the chairs have all the apparent obviousness of computer clip-art, but the unexpected cello leaves the whole sequence up for grabs. Beginning and ending in bubble-gum pink, the Day-Glo colouring of the series in between underlines the impression of comic-strip banality, to be called into question again by the musical instrument last in line. Like the Pop Art of the 1960s, Neo Pop is drawn to those miscellaneous shapes and images that for the most part pass the ordinary person by in a sort of cultural 'white noise'. Craig-Martin is fascinated by the odd accoutrements of everyday life, from office chairs like these, to mobile phones; things so familiar, he feels, you cannot depict the world without them.

CREATED

London

MEDIUM

Screen print

PERIOD/SERIES/MOVEMENT

Neo-Pop Art

SIMILAR WORKS

Haim Steinbach, *pink accent2*, 1987

Jeff Koons, *Grotto*, 2000

Michael Craig-Martin *Born* 1941 Dublin

Milroy, Lisa
Melons, 1986

Fruit was always the stuff of still life, from Zurburán to Gustave Courbet, but no old master ever represented fruit quite the way we see it here. This canvas highlights the fascination that Pop Art, both original and Neo, has found in visual reproduction and repetition – the melons here are arrayed rather as Andy Warhol would have done Elvises or Coca-Cola bottles. Except of course that here there is more spontaneity, and rather less mechanical regimentation. Still, the higgledy-piggledy arrangement really only underlines the artificiality of the scene.

This calls into question the apparent 'Realism' with which the melons are depicted: they are more about painterly tone and texture, in fact, than the imitation of nature. Just as in other apparently more outrageous works of recent art, what is being represented here is the process of representation and that related process by which art is created in the act, not of initial fashioning, but of final perception. The viewer in contemporary art is no mere audience, but is part of the artwork: 'The public is my ready-made,' remarked Jeff Koons in 1992.

CREATED

London

MEDIUM

Oil on canvas

PERIOD/SERIES/MOVEMENT

Neo-Pop Art

SIMILAR WORKS

Alan McCollum, *Lost Bones*, 1991

Julian Opie, *Fruit*, 2000

Lisa Milroy *Born* 1959 Vancouver, Canada,

Hirst, Damien

Painting for Marco Pierre-White, 1996

Courtesy of Jay Jopling/White Cube (London)/© the artist

Marcus Harvey's (b. 1963) *Myra* was *the* sensation of the Royal Academy's 'Sensation' exhibition of 1997. Gazing balefully out from beneath a great bob of peroxide hair in the infamous photograph, 'Moors Murderer' Myra Hindley was one of the great anti-icons of post-war Britain. Just to add insult to injury as far as many were concerned, Harvey's eleven-foot blow-up was composed entirely of children's hand prints.

Was this a calculated outrage? Ever since Damien Hirst launched the exhibition 'Freeze' in a warehouse in London's Docklands in 1988, there had been accusations that 'Britart' began and ended in cheap sensation. London's young artists made no attempt to reject the charge, making play with it instead. While works such as *Myra* and Tracey Emin's *Bed* became the lightning conductors for media-orchestrated outrage, others were getting on with only slightly less controversial work. Hirst himself, the founder of Britart, aroused press opprobrium for a series of animal carcasses bisected and preserved in formaldehyde, and this little still life is, in its way, just as challenging. Simultaneously charming and morbid, a memento mori and a record of cruelty, it sums up the aesthetic and moral ambiguity of great art.

CREATED

London

MEDIUM & DIMENSIONS

Gloss household paint and butterflies on canvas, 2 × 2 feet

PERIOD/SERIES/MOVEMENT

Britart/Young British Artists

SIMILAR WORKS

Tracey Emin, *Exploration of the Soul*, 1994

Damien Hirst *Born* 1965 Bristol, England

Modern Art

Landscape & Cityscape

Dufy, Raoul
The Three Umbrellas, 1906

Raoul Dufy had already achieved some standing as an Impressionist painter when, in 1906, he underwent a Road-to-Damascus conversion. The occasion of this great event was his first encounter with Henri Matisse's (1868–1954) *Luxe, Calme et Volupté* ('Luxury, calm and delight', a phrase from a Baudelaire poem). Matisse's masterpiece, one of the culminating works of his Neo-Impressionist period, had many of the characteristics of what would come to be known as 'Fauvist' painting. It was, Dufy marvelled, a 'miracle of creative imagination in colour and line', and colour and line became the main preoccupations of his own 'creative imagination' in his work thereafter. As an Impressionist, Dufy would have attempted a quasi-photographic reproduction of this riverside scene: Impressionism was a highly realistic school, despite its superficial messiness. Here, however, the colours and curves of the umbrellas become the centre of a swirling semi-abstract symphony in paint; the human forms are not only secondary, but almost disembodied, just parts of the pattern. 'Colours became charges of dynamite ... Everything could be raised above the real ...', as André Derain would remark later of the Fauvist school.

CREATED

Paris

MEDIUM

Oil on canvas

PERIOD/SERIES/MOVEMENT

Fauvism

SIMILAR WORKS

André Derain, *London: St Paul's Cathedral Seen from the Thames*, 1906

Raoul Dufy *Born* 1877 Le Havre, France

Died 1953.

Kirchner, Ernst Ludwig

Friedrichstrasse, 1914

'What is great about man is that he is a bridge and not a goal,' wrote philosopher Friedrich Nietzsche. It was this thought that prompted the foundation of *Die Brücke* or 'The Bridge' group in Dresden in 1905. Kirchner, the leader of this little movement, seems to have seen himself and his companions as bridging the gap between an exhausted past and a bright and energetic future: 'As youth we carry the future,' he declared in a strident manifesto.

The grandiosity of all this fanfare should not be allowed to obscure the genuine ambition of the Expressionist approach to art that Kirchner was articulating: 'Everybody belongs to our cause who reproduces directly and passionately what urges him to create,' he wrote. In truth, what urged him to create seems not to have been so much his sense of his youthful generation's destiny, as his own troubled childhood, racked by anxiety and tormented by nightmares.

The work shown here is typical, with its jagged slashes of lurid colour and distorted forms; the fashionably dressed streetwalkers of Friedrichstrasse have been elongated into serpent-like symbols of sexual temptation.

CREATED

Berlin

MEDIUM

Oil on canvas

PERIOD/SERIES/MOVEMENT

Expressionism/*Die Brücke*

SIMILAR WORKS

Erich Heckel, *Stralsund*, 1912

Ernst Ludwig Kirchner *Born* 1880 Aschaffenburg, Germany

Died 1938

Luks, George
Hester Street, 1905

'Art cannot be separated from life,' observed Robert Henri (1865–1929), famous as the founder of what would become known as New York Realism, in a half-facetious allusion to the down-and-dirty subject matter its practitioners chose. All is relative, of course – by the standards of the sort of 'Social Realism' produced later in America and Europe, much of the work of these painters now strikes us as cosy and picturesque. Unfortunately, life and art are all too easily separated in their work: Luks, for instance, did move in raffish, even squalid circles, and seems to have died in a street brawl. Few painters have 'embraced life' more incautiously, but his art is altogether tamer. Look beyond the racy subject matter of his street and saloon scenes, and you see an almost academic decorum in his work.

Even if the New York Realist school was artistically less radical than its beliefs, it should not be dismissed out of hand. Scenes like this one, showing market traders in Manhattan's Lower East Side, give a real sense of the hustle and bustle of life at street level.

CREATED

New York

MEDIUM

Oil on canvas

PERIOD/SERIES/MOVEMENT

New York Realism/Ashcan School

SIMILAR WORKS

Robert Henri, *Snow in New York*, 1902

George Luks *Born* 1867 Williamsport, PA, USA

Died 1933

Lawson, Ernest

Harlem River at Night, Blue Reflection, c. 1908

Courtesy of Private Collection, Christie's Images/www.bridgeman.co.uk/© Estate of Ernest Lawson

A friend and disciple of Robert Henri, Ernest Lawson belonged to the first group that this charismatic figure founded, known as 'The Eight' from the number of its members. However, Lawson was never really a signed-up member of the New York Realists. This is hardly surprising: Lawson was by training an Impressionist, attuned to the delicate play of light across land and water. By temperament, he was an old-fashioned romantic. Even when he embraced the democratic spirit of the Ashcan artists he remained aloof, seeking out the most solitary places he could find amid the city's hum. So, sympathetic as he was to the aims of the New York Realists, his works had little in common with theirs, except perhaps with John Sloan (1871–1951) in his most reflective mood. Lawson's tastes, his talents and his limitations are all summed up in this beautiful if unadventurous nocturne, clearly reminiscent of earlier works by James Abbott McNeill Whistler (1834–1903) and Claude Monet (1840–1926). Yet he should not be judged too harshly. His New York Realist colleagues were also less revolutionary than they imagined, but both helped establish the urban scene as a fitting subject for American art.

CREATED

New York

MEDIUM

Oil on canvas

PERIOD/SERIES/MOVEMENT

Impressionism/New York Realism/Ashcan School

SIMILAR WORKS

Maurice B. Prendergast, *Festival Night, Venice*, 1898–99

Ernest Lawson *Born* 1873 Halifax, Canada

Died 1939

Braque, Georges
Houses at L'Estaque, 1908

Georges Braque was the co-founder of Cubism along with Pablo Picasso, and for a few years around 1910 their works were almost indistinguishable. The 'Cubist' title is in some ways misleading, as few works have quite the block-like way with landscape as the studies that Braque made around his summer home at L'Estaque in southern France. What made the Cubists radical was their conscious attempt to attain a sense of depth by coming at their subjects from plural perspectives simultaneously. A contemporary critic, Louis Vauxcelles, stated that Braque 'despises form and reduces everything, landscapes and figures and houses, to geometric patterns, to cubes'. The accusation is understandable but unjust. The details here may be disregarded (no doors or windows in the houses, no leaves on the trees) – Braque does not even distinguish between the houses and the hills that surround them – yet he makes strenuous efforts to give a sense of reality in terms of palpable mass and three-dimensional depth. His is admittedly an intellectualized view of nature, but one with all the more integrity for that: 'The senses deform, the mind forms,' he believed.

CREATED

Paris

MEDIUM

Oil on canvas

PERIOD/SERIES/MOVEMENT

Cubism

SIMILAR WORKS

Pablo Picasso, *The Harvesters*, 1906

Georges Braque *Born* 1882 Le Havre, France

Died 1963

Severini, Gino
North–South, 1912

Strip away the proto-Fascist bombast from the Futurist philosophy, and comparatively little may be left. What does remain, however, is artistically worthwhile. In particular, the Futurists' concern to capture not the 'fixed moment' in a dynamic reality but the dynamic principle itself, makes sense as a challenge to be faced by the modern artist. Had the works of Marinetti never been written, this painting by Gino Severini would still stir the spirit with its depiction of a crowded and chaotic urban scene all but exploding with energy.

Set this work outside its immediate Futurist context and a French Cubist influence becomes apparent, which is underlined here, of course, by the Parisian setting. So too, on the other hand, is the formative inspiration that Wyndham Lewis's (1882–1957) Vorticism was to find in Futurism, although the two movements were very quickly to diverge. Overall it would be fair to say that the passage of time has treated the works of the Futurists well, freeing them from their unfortunate rhetorical baggage and allowing them to be judged by their own (often considerable) merits as works of art.

CREATED

Paris

MEDIUM

Oil on canvas

PERIOD/SERIES/MOVEMENT

Futurism

SIMILAR WORKS

Umberto Boccioni, *La Strada Entra nella Casa*, 1911

Gino Severini *Born* 1883 Cortona, Italy

Died 1966

Münter, Gabriele

Village Street in Winter, 1911

Courtesy of The Art Archive/Städtische Galerie im Lenbachhaus Munich/Dagli Orti/© Estate of Gabriele Munter

A student of Wassily Kandinsky (1866–1944) and for many years his lover (although never his artistic emulator), Gabriele Münter became a leading light of the *Neue Künstlervereinigung München* ('New Artists' Association of Munich' or NKV). Founded in 1909, the NKV was not strictly speaking a school or movement: its purpose was to provide a venue for exhibiting works that fell foul of the city's highly conservative artistic establishment. Certain shared values did emerge, however. In particular the French Fauves had a major impact, seen in this cityscape, with its out-of-kilter structures and crazy colour scheme. Münter's bold strokes and childlike composition could hardly have contrasted more starkly with the elegant sophistication and subtle tones of *Jugendstil*, the German version of Art Nouveau, still in vogue. Respectable citizens flocked to NKV exhibitions just to register contempt – one dealer had to wipe the spit from the canvases every night. Ironically, though, the movement would be a casualty of its own conservatism. When one of his pictures was rejected for exhibition in 1911, Kandinsky formed the rival *Der Blaue Reiter* ('Blue Rider') group, which effectively eclipsed it.

CREATED

Munich

MEDIUM

Oil on canvas

PERIOD/SERIES/MOVEMENT

Neue Künstlervereinigung München

SIMILAR WORKS

Alexei von Jawlensky, *Landscape with Red Roof, c.* 1911

Gabriele Münter *Born* 1877 Berlin, Germany

Died 1962

de Chirico, Giorgio
The Mystery and Melancholy of a Street, 1914

'We who understand the signs of the metaphysical alphabet know what joys and sorrows are hidden within a portico, the angle of a street.' Giorgio de Chirico built a city of symbols in his art. By tradition emblems of order and regularity, the 'classical' arches, columns and statues he favoured in his work hinted ironically at the limits of human reason and the irreducible unknown that lay beyond. It was up to art to explore this realm, at least implicitly, he felt. Accordingly, around 1913, he formulated the philosophy of his *Pittura Metafisica* ('Metaphysical Painting'). 'To become truly immortal,' he wrote, 'a work of art must escape all human limits: logic and common sense will only interfere.' Carlo Carrà promptly consigned his Futurism to the past in his eagerness to follow him, although the two would part company again a few years later.

The Mystery and Melancholy of a Street is an utterly extraordinary work, inexpressibly haunting and yet its compositional components are strikingly familiar. Walking the frontier between figure and shadow, physical reality and thought, it offers a scary, uplifting glimpse into infinite space.

CREATED

Paris

MEDIUM

Oil on canvas

PERIOD/SERIES/MOVEMENT

Pittura Metafisica

SIMILAR WORKS

Alexei von Jawlensky, *Paesaggio*, 1911

Giorgio de Chirico *Born* 1888 Volo, Greece, 1888

Died 1978

Delaunay, Robert

Triomphe de Paris, 1928–29

'As for our work,' wrote Robert Delaunay to Wassily Kandinsky in 1912, 'I think that surely the public will have to get used to it. The effort it will have to make comes slowly because it is drowned in habits.' In truth, the art-loving public would never really feel at home with Orphism, in theory at least; in practice, paradoxically, it was easy to relate to.

Named after Orpheus, the lyre-playing bard of Greek legend, Orphism was originally a tendency within French Cubism. It was identified around 1912 by a non-painter, the poet Apollinaire: the fact that it was arguably projected on to the art of Delaunay and his circle by an outsider did not make it any easier to understand. The Orphists themselves embraced the label gladly, although quite what it meant was never certain, beyond the fact that it sought to offset the diagrammatic quality of Cubism with a lyric touch and to attain the 'purity' of expression, unencumbered by meaning, to be found in music. Fortunately there was no need to fathom the thinking to appreciate Orphic painting, which was often, as here, a wonderful symphony of shape and colour.

CREATED

Paris

MEDIUM

Oil on canvas

PERIOD/SERIES/MOVEMENT

Orphism

SIMILAR WORKS

Frantisek Kupka, *Vertical and Horizontal Planes*, c. 1913–14

Robert Delaunay *Born* 1885 Paris, France

Died 1941

Popova, Ljubov

Fabrika Iaschikov ('The Box Factory'), 1913–14

'Down with art! Long live technology!' was one of the cries of Constructivism. This picture may promote technological values but it is very clearly art. There's an air of great excitement about this canvas, but a vague suggestion of caricature too: what could possibly have made a more stereotypically appropriate subject for a Constructivist artist than an industrial plant built for the purpose of manufacturing boxes, principally cardboard cubes?

The daughter of a wealthy Russian family, Popova had in fact been a card-carrying Cubist, working with Le Fauconnier and others in Paris, before obeying the Constructivist call to arms in the aftermath of revolution in her homeland. Her work illustrates many of the movement's strengths: there is a sense of indomitable energy and movement about this crowded canvas and a real feel of dimension and of depth. Yet, when all is said and done, it is hard to avoid a suspicion that the real success of this painting lies in Popova's more bourgeois and old-fashioned artistic virtues: most important, of course, is the richness of her colour tones.

CREATED

Moscow

MEDIUM

Gouache and pencil on paper

PERIOD/SERIES/MOVEMENT

Cubism/Constructivism

SIMILAR WORKS

Alexandra Exter, *Construction*, 1922–23

Varvara Stepanova, *Figure*, 1921

Ljubov Popova *Born* 1889 near Moscow, Russia

Died 1924

Tatlin, Vladimir Evgrafovich
Monument to the Third International, 1919–20

No work better encapsulates the heroic ambition of the Soviet experiment than Vladimir Tatlin's *Monument to the Third International*, nor does any better embody its final failure. The leaning edifice of iron and glass, as originally envisaged, was to rise far higher than the Eiffel Tower and far beyond the resources and expertise of Soviet Russia at that time.

Consequently this 'Soviet Tower of Babel' was never to be built, although the gigantic model that was made was an impressive work of sculpture in its own right. Even so, it would not be without its detractors. The most trenchant criticism came from renegade Constructivist Naum Gabo, who said it was 'not pure Constructivist art, but merely an imitation of the machine'. The objection is a revealing one, but it highlights a problem as old as Marxist aesthetics: how does one find an art that not only represents, but also actually *embodies* a dynamic revolutionary drive? The problem was to bedevil Soviet art and literature: what became known as 'Socialist Realism' canonized work of crashing conventionality, even conservatism, just so long as it glorified the workers and the Communist cause.

CREATED

Moscow

MEDIUM

Lithograph, showing iron model

PERIOD/SERIES/MOVEMENT

Constructivism

SIMILAR WORKS

El Lissitzky, *Untitled*, c. 1919–20

Vladimir Evgrafovich Tatlin Born 1885 Kharkov, Ukraine

Died 1953

Rodchenko, Alexsandr Mikhajlovich
The Construction of the USSR, c. 1920

Courtesy of Museum of the Revolution, Moscow, Russia, Giraudon/www.bridgeman.co.uk/© DACS 2005

From today's perspective, it is hard not to take a jaundiced view of a work that we know was helping to initiate a long and increasingly cynical tradition of Soviet Poster Art. Lenin's leadership was set to usher in the cult of personality on the one hand and the Gulag on the other, and the 'dictatorship of the proletariat' would end up ruthlessly suppressing the rights of the individual. Much of the technological and economic progress symbolized by the electrical pylon in this picture would indeed be made, but the human costs of progress under Stalin's Five-Year Plans would be severe.

Such objections are anachronistic, however, and entirely miss the point of a work that offers a genuinely idealistic, genuinely stirring summons to the workers and intellectuals, of what promised, not altogether unconvincingly, to be a Utopian state. It is itself 'constructed' in collage form from mechanically created images, rather than by more traditional techniques such as drawing or painting. Unfortunately in rejecting 'bourgeois art' and its values so vehemently, Soviet artists threw the artistic baby out with the bourgeois bath water, opening the door to decades of banality and Philistinism.

CREATED

Moscow

MEDIUM

Collage

PERIOD/SERIES/MOVEMENT

Constructivism

SIMILAR WORKS

El Lissitzky, *Beat the Whites with the Red Wedge*, 1919

Alexsandr Mikhajlovich Rodchenko *Born* 1891 St Petersburg, Russia

Died 1956

Höch, Hannah

Rome, 1925

The use of 'readymade' materials had been a part of Dadaist thinking from the very outset. It was felt that artistic creativity lay in the inspiration, which wrested such items from their original purpose. In the years after the First World War an increasing interest was shown in ready-made images, and Hannah Höch is usually credited with the introduction of photomontage.

'Our whole purpose,' she said in a later interview, 'was to integrate objects from the world of machines and industry in the world of art. Our typographical collages or montages set out to achieve this by imposing, on something which could only be produced by hand, the appearances of something that had been entirely composed by a machine.' Where Futurists and Constructivists celebrated machinery and industrialism for their driving, depersonalized power, Höch sees technology as an aspect of human creativity. The distinction may be subtle, but it is significant: where the Futurists ended up in hock to Fascism and the Constructivists to Communism, Höch remained aloof from the totalitarian drive and would never fit comfortably into the Nazi scheme of things.

CREATED

Berlin

MEDIUM

Oil on canvas with photomontage

PERIOD/SERIES/MOVEMENT

Dadaism

SIMILAR WORKS

Raoul Hausmann, *The Art Critic*, 1919–20

Hannah Höch *Born* 1889 Gotha, Germany

Died 1978

Feininger, Lyonel

Ssenborn, 1923

Born in America to a family of German origin, Feininger went to Europe as a young man to study music, a love he never lost although drawn by degrees into the artistic life of Hamburg and Berlin. During a spell in Paris he first encountered the paintings of the French Cubists, whose influence would thereafter be apparent in his own work. A political caricaturist of genius, his command of the line was perfect, but as a painter he was fascinated by the play of light across interlocking planes. He found the perfect subject in the angled rooftops, walls and church spires of Thuringian villages, such as Ssenborn, not far from Weimar.

Feininger is not easily categorized as a painter. A co-founder of Walter Gropius's Bauhaus in 1919, he subsequently joined Kandinsky, Paul Klee (1879–1940) and Alexei Jawlensky (1864–1941) as one of *Die Blaue Vier* ('The Blue Four'). In truth this was really an entrepreneurial bid on the part of four confirmed mavericks, with little in common but independent mindedness, for the sort of the promotional possibilities available to the more cohesive and readily identifiable artistic 'school'.

CREATED

Weimar

MEDIUM

Oil on canvas

PERIOD/SERIES/MOVEMENT

Die Blaue Vier ('The Blue Four')

SIMILAR WORKS

Paul Klee, *Red Villa Quarter*, 1920

Lyonel Feininger *Born* 1871 New York, USA

Died 1956

Ernst, Max

The Embalmed Forest, 1933

Max Ernst was every bit as eccentric as might be expected of a Surrealist painter, often talking of himself in the third person, for example. He also figured in many of his own pictures (as here) in the person of 'Laplop', a strange stylized bird. This identification appears to have originated in a traumatic event of his early childhood, when his baby sister died on the same day as a beloved pet bird. In this disturbing dream scene, a circular rising moon touches the canopy of a dark forest with its eerie light, while tree trunks lean hither and thither at crazy angles. At first glance the trees seem crudely daubed, but closer inspection reveals a silvery filigree, which produces an almost palpable texture.

Ernst cared about the 'feel' of his works: he had invented the artistic technique of frottage: rubbing over ridged surfaces such as wood or stone with charcoal to reveal the hidden patterns. His interest lay partly in the element of chance. Like other Surrealists, he set great store by the random and unplanned, but he also evidently responded to the physicality of such materials.

CREATED

Paris

MEDIUM

Oil on canvas

PERIOD/SERIES/MOVEMENT

Surrealism

SIMILAR WORKS

André Masson, *Battle of Fishes*, 1927

Max Ernst *Born* 1891 Cologne, Germany

Died 1976

Tanguy, Yves
Les Nouveaux Nomads, 1935

Legend has it that Yves Tanguy was travelling on a bus one day in 1923 when he glimpsed a picture by Giorgio de Chirico in a shop window. Leaping from the moving vehicle in his eagerness to look more closely, he was lucky to escape with his life, a life he decided thereupon would be dedicated to painting. By 1925 he was a member of the Surrealist circle surrounding André Breton (1896–1966).

Whatever the truth of the story, there is no doubt that Tanguy was a latecomer to serious art, and that he was essentially an autodidact, without formal training. Could the layman's residual sense of the duty of art to be representative, in a literalistic sort of way, be why his weirdest canvases are still executed with the closest attention to detail? Or is it just the interplay of imaginative extravagance and matter-of-fact meticulousness that appealed? The tension between the mundane and the marvellous can be seen at the centre of all great art. It is certainly to be seen in the Surrealist art of Salvador Dali (1904–1989), who brought a finicky scrupulousness to some of the strangest paintings ever seen.

CREATED

Paris

MEDIUM

Oil on canvas

PERIOD/SERIES/MOVEMENT

Surrealism

SIMILAR WORKS

Salvador Dali, *The Persistence of Memory*, 1931

Yves Tanguy *Born* 1900 Paris, France

Died 1955

Miró, Joan

Mythologization of Landscape (Dialogue of Insects), 1924–25

Catalan genius Joan Miró was 'the most surrealistic of us all,' according to André Breton, but he was one of the movement's least doctrinaire, most wayward adherents. The dream-like quality of his canvases makes the 'Surrealist' label inevitable, and justifiable, as far as it goes. Still, there is more to Miró than it implies in some ways and in other ways less: more, because his individual talent obviously transcended the strictures of any school, but less because he was largely indifferent to the elaborate theories that the true-believing Surrealists kept developing. He was also willing to 'cheat', in Surrealist terms, for the effects he required. His own integrity was his ruling guide: 'What really counts is to strip the soul naked,' he once said. But that 'soul' was a calculating, contriving one: where serious Surrealists resorted to techniques like frottage or automatic painting to sidestep the workings of the conscious mind, he worked with fanatic precision to a careful plan. All apparent abandon and naïveté, his great works were consummate in their discipline: 'right to the millimetre,' he declared with pride.

CREATED

Paris or Montroig, Spain

MEDIUM

Oil on canvas

PERIOD/SERIES/MOVEMENT

Surrealism

Joan Miró *Born* 1893 Barcelona, Spain

Died 1983

Utrillo, Maurice

Sacré Coeur, Montmartre, 1937

The School of Paris, as American critic Harold Rosenberg observed, belonged to no one country: rather, it was 'world-wide, world-timed and pertinent everywhere ...'. Maurice Utrillo was not the school's most illustrious alumnus, perhaps, but he was the creator of many entrancing works and a living symbol of the spirit prevailing in early twentieth-century Paris. It was a cosmopolitan spirit and a warmly welcoming one to the world's outsiders: Utrillo himself was the illegitimate son of artist Suzanne Valadon. He was formally adopted by the Spanish painter Miguel Utrillo, hence his dual-nationality name, out of what appears to have been sheer altruism. Despite this kindly intervention, his was undoubtedly a challenging childhood, with Maurice Utrillo an alcoholic by his early teenage years. It made sense, then, for him to join with Amedeo Modigliani (1884–1920), Jules Pascin (1885–1930) and Chaïm Soutine (1893–1943) as one of *Les Maudits* ('The Accursed') – yet his works give the impression of a painter always happy to count his blessings. Many of his works were street scenes, painted in his home district of Montmartre. Although indefatigably cheerful, they venture beyond the picturesque.

CREATED

Paris

MEDIUM

Oil on canvas

PERIOD/SERIES/MOVEMENT

École de Paris ('School of Paris')

SIMILAR WORKS

Amedeo Modigliani, *Cypress Trees and Houses*

Maurice Utrillo *Born* 1883 Paris, France

Died 1955

Église Saint ... de Montmartre.

Maurice Utrillo, V.
Avril 1937.

Grosz, George
'Beauty' from *Ecce Homo*, 1923

Launched in the 1920s, the *Neue Sachlichkeit* ('New Objectivity') movement set out to portray modern society in all its decadence and corruption. In addition to George Grosz, it included other German painters such as Käthe Kollwitz (the movement's pioneer), Max Beckmann and Otto Dix. The title of Grosz's portfolio, *Ecce Homo* ('Behold the Man'), is a reference to Friedrich Nietzsche's autobiography, whose philosophy had particular currency at the time. The guilt regarding the state of mankind did not all lie at the door of humanity, however: 'My pictures are a reproach to God for all that he does wrong,' said Beckmann. Nor did 'Objectivity' imply straightforward 'Realism'. In fact these painters favoured a shockingly unfunny form of caricature, depicting their subjects not as they appeared, but as they were morally: ugly grotesques. Here a nude woman in a café suggests a society stripped bare; she wears only stockings, a fur stole, a choker and jewelled earrings, not clothing but the marks of material wealth. Her face is made-up, her body naked: a symbol of sex for sale, while ugly-mugged businessmen sit around, clothed in respectability.

CREATED

Berlin

MEDIUM

Watercolour

PERIOD/SERIES/MOVEMENT

Neue Sachlichkeit ('New Objectivity')

SIMILAR WORKS

Käthe Kollwitz, *The Widow I, c.* 1922–24

George Grosz *Born* 1893 Berlin, Germany

Died 1959

Dix, Otto

Pragerstrasse ('Prague Street'), 1920

This horrific canvas was created in the immediate aftermath of the First World War, from which many thousands of German men had come home grotesquely mutilated. This is a truly shocking work in which satirical anger outweighs compassion, with Dix portraying his veterans as semi-monsters.

One trundles along on a wheeled board, no more than a grinning automaton; another begs outside a shop window like a giant spider. The displays behind him offer ironic comment on his condition – the artificial limbs to one side echoing his own amputations and the wigs and corsets showing how war's butchery is burlesqued in the name of beauty. A fashionable lady passes by with a little dog: her own body crudely cut by the edge of the scene, we see only a buttock covered by a clinging skirt. Her absurd boots pick up the overall theme of the distortions imposed by the pursuit of power on the one hand and by vanity on the other. To bottom left, a snarling dog holds out a leaflet bearing the slogan *Juden raus!* ('Jews out!'): this is a society in the throes of self-dismemberment.

CREATED

Düsseldorf

MEDIUM

Oil on canvas

PERIOD/SERIES/MOVEMENT

Neue Sachlichkeit ('New Objectivity')

SIMILAR WORKS

George Grosz, *The Pillars of Society*, 1926

Otto Dix *Born* 1891 Thuringia, Germany, 1891

Died 1969

Delvaux, Paul

La Ville Inquiète ('The Anxious Town'), 1941

Belgian painter Paul Delvaux was a relative latecomer to Surrealism, but he embraced the creed with all the convert's zeal. His work was of the type that would eventually become known as 'Magic Realism', since it seemed less simply nonsensical than more stereotypically Surrealist art. Also, although its final inexplicability was clearly central to Delvaux's project, his works always seemed to hint at a sort of hazy narrative sense. Delvaux was a deeply paradoxical painter: his work may have been profoundly experimental, yet in its visual components it was in many ways conservative. He shared with the western artists of many centuries a fascination with the human form, populating his paintings with nude figures very much in the Classical tradition. Many of his cityscapes are Classical in appearance too: here, albeit distantly, we see colonnades and temples in the Greek or Roman style. Context is all, however, and Delvaux's men and women are characteristically deployed in scenes of mystery: often they stare into space, as though entranced. Here an extra dimension of mystery is added by the presence of a scattering of figures suited like twentieth-century office workers, possibly self-portraits of the artist.

CREATED

Brussels

MEDIUM

Oil on canvas

PERIOD/SERIES/MOVEMENT

Magic Realism/Surrealism

SIMILAR WORKS

Giorgio de Chirico, *The Enigma of a Day*, 1914

Paul Delvaux *Born* 1891 near Liège, Belgium

Died 1994

Tooker, George
Government Bureau, 1956

'Magical', 'charming', 'enchanting': words such as these have become terms of critical endearment, yet magic was originally a decidedly sinister thing. We do well to remember this when we come to consider what is known as 'Magical Realism'. There is nothing cosy or reassuring about this painting by the American artist George Tooker, and neither could this conceivably be described as an 'escapist' work.

Quite the contrary, indeed: if this scene is extraordinary, it is only because it multiplies ordinariness to the nth degree. The eerie effect is achieved by replication: more or less identical members of the public queuing up before more or less identical windows to be directed by more or less identical officials. Government is strictly demarcated from the public it nominally represents, its clerks half-glimpsed behind distorting glass, while regimented beams and light fittings recede into the distance. The stooped figure in the foreground seems marooned in modern life: he exudes isolation and alienation; social conformity leaves the individual high and dry. A simple work, without a hint of the exotic or the overstated about it, yet the impression it makes could hardly be more powerful.

CREATED

New York

MEDIUM

Egg tempera on gesso panel

PERIOD/SERIES/MOVEMENT

Magic Realism

SIMILAR WORKS

Peter Blume, *South of Scranton*, 1931

George Tooker *Born* 1920 Brooklyn, New York, USA

Wood, Grant
Stone City, 1930

The American Midwest in 1930 was not quite the idyllic scene we see before us here, with the region reeling from a sixty per cent slump in grain prices. Although associated with the 1930s, the Great Depression had struck agricultural America rather earlier, and the Dust Bowl was just around the corner. Ostensibly 'Realist' in style, the paintings of the Regionalists were clearly idealizations, as fantastical in their way as any of the creations of the Surrealists. The philosophy underpinning them was a rejection of European decadence and avant-garde aesthetics in favour of an honest-to-goodness Americanism and homely simplicity. Their appeal to a nation sinking ever deeper into economic crisis is easy enough to understand – they represented nostalgia for a time of prosperity gone by. As political instability gripped a Europe where Communism and Fascism were on the march, a scene of peace and order like this one was profoundly reassuring. A genuine farm boy from rural Iowa, Grant Wood was largely self-taught as an artist, but he did make several visits to Europe and studied for a time in Paris.

CREATED

Cedar Rapids, Iowa

MEDIUM

Oil on canvas

PERIOD/SERIES/MOVEMENT

Regionalism

SIMILAR WORKS

Thomas Hart Benton, *Haystack*, 1938

Grant Wood *Born* 1892 Iowa, USA

Died 1942

Edward Hopper
Chop Suey, 1929

The terms 'American Scene' and 'Regionalism' are often used interchangeably and, from a technical point of view, this makes perfect sense. Some artists stayed aloof from what became an ideologically freighted Regionalism, however, and the American Scene description is better reserved for them. Edward Hopper's accounts of an everyday America are peculiarly unsettling. He shows a nation cut off from its productive countryside and from those wide-open spaces celebrated by the Regionalists. Here, sunlight barely makes it through the painted-glass window of an urban restaurant. Reflected from a bare white table, it casts a sickly pallor over the lady facing us: Hopper's figures frequently seem like spectres, making their way through the world like the living dead. Isolated, wrapped up in themselves, they come together in anonymous, transitional locations – motel rooms, diners, deserted offices – conversing without ever apparently making contact. Modernism has romanticized the rootless nature of urban society, seeing something heroic in the individual alone, but Hopper had many of the same hankerings as his Regionalist contemporaries. Set against an ideal of community, of social co-operation, a work such as this one is a vision of the damned.

CREATED

New York

MEDIUM

Oil on canvas

PERIOD/SERIES/MOVEMENT

American Scene

Edward Hopper *Born* 1882 Nyack, NY, USA

Died 1967

Soyer, Raphael

Café Scene

Raphael Soyer came to America as a young teenager when his family emigrated from Russia in 1913, and his twin brother Moses was also destined to become an important artist. Along with a deep gratitude to their host country, they brought with them a spirit of European radicalism, an inheritance shared by their fellow immigrant, the Lithuanian Ben Shahn. All three came of age artistically at a time when increasing numbers of home-grown Americans were reacting against Regionalism with its nationalistic pieties and its unstated agenda of political conservatism. Painters such as Reginald Marsh and Isabel Bishop were making a common cause with a new breed of documentary photographers like Margaret Bourke-White in offering a new and unsparing portrait of a less than ideal society. 'Yes,' said Moses Soyer, 'paint America, but with your eyes open. Do not glorify Main Street. Paint it as it is – mean, dirty, avaricious.'

His brother in fact painted few street scenes, glorified or otherwise, being more interested in the way social reality impacted on individual psychology: this solitary, introspective woman is characteristic of his work.

CREATED

New York

MEDIUM

Oil on canvas

PERIOD/SERIES/MOVEMENT

Social Realism

SIMILAR WORKS

Reginald Marsh, *Subway, 14th Street*, 1930

Raphael Soyer *Born* 1899 Borisoglebsk, Russia

Died 1987

Gropper, William

Youngstown Strike, c. 1937

Courtesy of Butler Institute of American Art, Youngstown, OH, USA, Museum Purchase 1985/www.bridgeman.co.uk/© Estrate of William Gropper

This picture was painted in the 1930s at a time when industrial unrest had all America in its grip, including the Sheet and Tube Company of Youngstown, Ohio. Yet it depicted an earlier episode: the moment in 1916 when strikers at the Youngstown plant had been fired upon by police guards; three had been killed and many others wounded. The painting's sympathies are clear – it makes its subject not just heroic but historic, conferring epic status on the workers' struggle. The simplicity of the figures in thick impasto seem paradoxically modern and 'primitivist', but their postures and gestures recall the 'Roman' melodramas of Jacques-Louis David. Consciously or not, Gropper wished to create iconic images that would do for the labour movement what Emmanuel Leutze's *Washington Crossing the Delaware* (1851) had done for 'official' America.

Many Depression-era artists were explicitly partisan. The failure of capitalism seemed palpable, while the Soviet Union seemed to be going from strength to strength. In reality disillusion was just around the corner. Even as this picture was painted, Stalin was mounting his first show trials of opponents and negotiating the Nazi-Soviet Pact.

CREATED

New York

MEDIUM

Oil on canvas

PERIOD/SERIES/MOVEMENT

Social Realism

SIMILAR WORKS

Isabel Bishop, *Bootblack, c.* 1933

William Gropper *Born* 1897 New York, USA

Died 1977

Laktionov, Alexander

Letter from the Front, 1947

Courtesy of Tretyakov Gallery, Moscow, Russia/www.bridgeman.co.uk/© Estate of Alexander Laktionov

Works such as this were to win Laktionov the Stalin Prize in 1948 and, by 1969, the ultimate honorific title: that of 'People's Artist of the USSR'. They were also to bring down on him the contempt of the artistic world at large. Leaving aside the monstrous evil of the regime, which works like this were dedicated to glorifying, 'Socialist Realism' became a byword for banality. It might be felt that revolutionary times call for revolutionary art. Indeed the Russian Revolution had found such a spirit in the Constructivists, however misguided they may seem in hindsight. Yet the aesthetic promoted by the Soviet state was profoundly conservative and conformist in its intentions, as a directive of 1934 made all too clear. 'Artistic portrayal must be in harmony with the objective of the ideological alteration and education of the workers,' the statute said: the artist's role was as a sort of creative commissar.

It has been pointed out with some justice that American Regionalism offered an analogous 'Capitalist Realism', just as pious and just as fatuous – it was just that the Soviet version was imposed under threat of the Gulag.

CREATED

Moscow

MEDIUM

Oil on canvas

PERIOD/SERIES/MOVEMENT

Socialist Realism

SIMILAR WORKS

Sergei Alekseevich Grigorev, *Admission into the Komsomol,* 1949

Alexander Laktionov *Born* 1910 Rostov-on-Don, Russia

Died 1972

Lowry, L. S.
The Canal Bridge, 1949

One of modern Britain's best-loved painters, L. S. Lowry was unapproachable in person; he painted happy crowds, but was himself a sad and solitary figure. He was isolated geographically too, spending his whole life in Manchester, well away from metropolitan London where the cultural running was supposedly being made. Despite this he was anything but parochial in his attitude to art. Neither was he the self-taught genius of legend: he studied intermittently yet seriously for over 20 years, many of them under the tutelage of the French painter Adolphe Valette (1876–1942).

Although his works betray the influence of the earlier Camden Town Group, his melancholy humour is all his own. He had a distinctive ambivalence towards his fellow men and women, whom he seems to have loved, but preferred in the undifferentiated anonymity of the crowd. He painted an urban industrial landscape that we are accustomed to regard as grim, but which in his work appears positively picturesque.

CREATED

Manchester

MEDIUM

Oil on canvas

SIMILAR WORKS

Robert Bevan, *Horse Dealers (Sale at Ward's Repository, No. 1)*, 1918

Charles Isaac Ginner, *Bethnal Green Allotment*, c. 1943

Laurence Stephen Lowry *Born* 1887 Manchester, England

Died 1976

Mathieu, Georges

Seventh Avenue, New York, 1957

Courtesy of Musee d'Unterlinden, Colmar, France, Lauros/Giraudon/www.bridgeman.co.uk/© Georges Mathieu

'Speed, intuition, excitement: that is my method of creation,' said Georges Mathieu of his style of painting. It was a style that did indeed privilege the act and energy of painting over the form of the finished product, which was deemed to have value only in so far as it could be seen as embodying that creative frenzy. The French name that was given to this approach, *Art Informel*, meant not just 'informal art' but, quite literally 'art without form'. The apparent oxymoron makes a sort of sense so long as the viewer is prepared to accept the premise that the artwork is the record of a process rather than a completed design. The movement's founder, Michel Tapié, had announced in 1952: 'Today, art must stupefy to be art.'

Art Informel certainly stupefied: exhibition-goers struggled to make sense of a genre that owed nothing either to traditional Realism or the avant garde departures of the pre-war years. Mathieu specialized in Tachism ('Stain-ism', from *tâche*, meaning 'stain' or 'blot'), in which the artist's unplanned mark on the canvas represented an assertion of his existence.

CREATED

Paris

MEDIUM

Oil on canvas

PERIOD/SERIES/MOVEMENT

Art Informel/Tachisme

SIMILAR WORKS

Wols (Alfred Otto Wolfgang Schulze), *Painting*, 1944–45

Hans Hartung, *Composition in Black and Yellow*, 1958

Georges Mathieu *Born* 1921 Boulogne, France

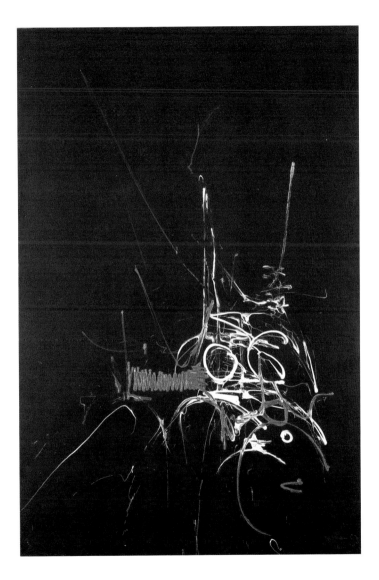

Kline, Franz

Provincetown II, 1959

'The final test of a painting ...', said Franz Kline, is 'Does the painter's emotion come across?' His works are intensely felt, even by the standards of Abstract Expressionism. This movement of the 1950s and 1960s rejected both Realism and the more geometric forms of abstract art: the painter's task was to represent not objects, scenes or patterns, but emotions. Kline saw his paintings as 'situations': his first brushstroke set in motion a drama that he then wrestled to resolve. The sense of struggle in his work is thrilling, and his most famous works seem like epic battles of black and white; only in his last years did he move to incorporate a much greater range of colours.

It had not always been thus: as a young man, Kline had gone to England to pursue a decorous interest in nineteenth-century illustration. His own works of the 1930s were of a piece with this – conservative, even genteel – but all that changed when he met Willem de Kooning (1904–97) in 1943. He was transfixed by the Dutchman's genius, and his own art was transformed: Kline became one of the boldest artists of his generation.

CREATED

New York

MEDIUM

Oil on canvas

PERIOD/SERIES/MOVEMENT

Abstract Expressionism

SIMILAR WORKS

Willem de Kooning, *Composition*, 1955

Franz Kline *Born* 1910 Wilkes-Barre, PA, USA

Died 1962

Hamilton, Richard

'Just What Is It That Makes Today's Homes So Different, So Appealing?', 1959

'Pop': so reads the logo on the lollipop being brandished like a phallus by Charles Atlas here. Did this work mark the foundation of the Pop Art movement? That claim may be disputed, as other London artists such as Peter Blake (b. 1923) and Joe Tilson (b. 1928) were working in a comparable style, but it was this collage that stole the show at the breakthrough 'This is Tomorrow' exhibition in 1956: it marked the birth both of a style and a sensibility. All the elements of Pop Art are present: the playful use of 'found' materials in montage; the delight in current commercial styles; the irreverence towards 'high' culture and the evident pleasure with which the work is made. The only real difference from what might be regarded as 'classic' Warhol-style Pop Art is the slight suggestion of a satirical edge. The body-builder husband and pin-up wife, the conspicuously well-appointed home – are we celebrating or sending up these aspirations? From the wall above the television, the Victorian art critic and social thinker John Ruskin looks down: we can only imagine what he must be thinking.

CREATED

London

MEDIUM

Collage

PERIOD/SERIES/MOVEMENT

Pop Art

SIMILAR WORKS

R. B. Kitaj, *The Murder of Rosa Luxemburg*, 1960

Richard Hamilton *Born* 1922 London, England

Frankenthaler, Helen
The Bay, 1963

'Stain painting' is one of several movements arguably spawned by Abstract Impressionism, but impatient with its overt emotionalism. Painters such as De Kooning, Kline and Mark Rothko had brought an almost religious intensity to their work, an earnestness with which a younger generation found itself uneasy. The 1950s had seen the coming of 'Cool Jazz' on to the music scene: elegant, mellow and effortlessly accomplished. Younger painters set out to embody those qualities in art.

Helen Frankenthaler found a way of letting the paint do all the work, pouring it directly on to the canvas, and then letting it spread out where it would. Where Jackson Pollock had poured thick paint, however, she thinned hers so that it would spread out more freely and be absorbed into the canvas, a technique to which she gave the name of 'soak-stain'. The difference is significant, with implications not only for the size of the resulting stain, but for the relationship between the paint and its background. The two interpenetrated in Frankenthaler's works, colour and canvas inseparably integrated to produce a somehow complete and satisfying work of art.

CREATED

New York

MEDIUM

Acrylic on canvas

PERIOD/SERIES/MOVEMENT

Post-painterly Abstraction/Green Mountain Boys

SIMILAR WORKS

Morris Louis, *Beth Chaf*, 1959

Kenneth Noland, *Half*, 1959

Helen Frankenthaler *Born* 1928 New York, USA

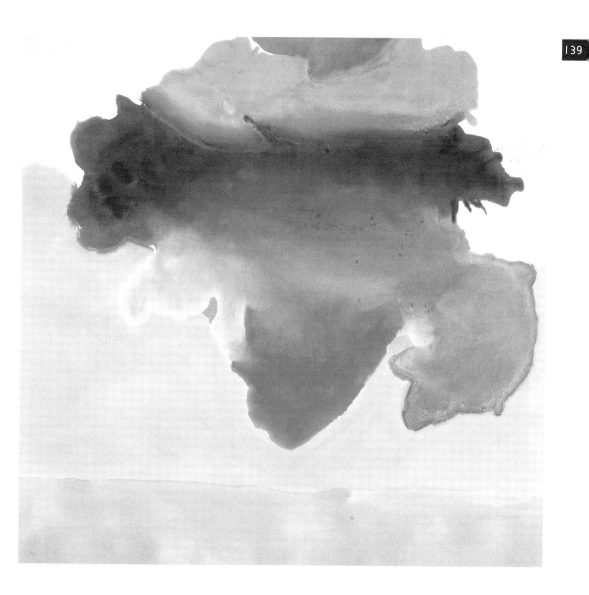

Estes, Richard

Boston Five Cents Savings Bank, 1974

Courtesy of Private Collection/www.bridgeman.co.uk/© Richard Estes, courtesy, Marlborough Gallery, New York

Apart from a few politically motivated movements, the whole tenor of development in twentieth-century art was moving away from naturalistic representation: why then the emergence of Superrealism (or 'Photorealism', or 'Hyperrealism') in the late 1960s? Why would gifted artists labour long and hard simply to recreate effects of a sort that could be achieved so effortlessly by the use of photography? The movement makes more sense if Superrealism is understood, not as the ultimate in imitation of the old-fashioned kind, but as the modern concern with surfaces taken to extremes. Far from being more restrained than the more obviously exotic works of Pop Art, these fake photos represent art at its most self-consciously artificial. No slavish copies of reality, they are outrageous ironic commentaries upon it.

Estes' images of reflective glass are a bravura feature in his work, but they represent more than mere virtuosity. They show the creation and distortion of light and space within the work of art. Like Dadaist creations carried to their logical conclusion, they make a 'found' object of the environment as a whole.

CREATED

New York

MEDIUM

Acrylic on board

PERIOD/SERIES/MOVEMENT

Superrealism

SIMILAR WORKS

Malcolm Morley, *Beach Scene*, 1969

Richard Estes *Born* 1936 Kewanee, IL, USA

Salt, John

Pink Trailer With Plymouth, 1974

Courtesy of Wolverhampton Art Gallery, West Midlands, UK/www.bridgeman.co.uk/© John Salt

'All flesh is grass', goes the Biblical adage; the work of John Salt offers an updated version: 'all cars are scrap'. What the grinning skull was for medieval art, an eloquently silent *memento mori*, Salt's car and caravan do here for a consumerist age.

It is interesting to note that the British-born artist went out to America in 1967, and as a creator of abstractions, he subsequently adopted Superrealism as a conscious choice. His works in the style have been varied, depicting everything from street scenes to industrial installations, but cars have been a recurrent theme. Not, however, for the most part, as moving vehicles and symbols of mechanical strength and speed, but as static objects, whether parked or, as here, abandoned. Such images clearly have something to say about the values of the modern throwaway society, but most viewers will find a deeper melancholy here. The comparison with Hopper has been made: these rusting vehicles are the discarded shells of empty existences, without roots, without purpose, perhaps ultimately without meaning.

CREATED

New York

MEDIUM

Oil on canvas

PERIOD/SERIES/MOVEMENT

Superrealism

SIMILAR WORKS

Robert Bechtle, *'60 T-Bird*, 1967–68

John Salt *Born* 1937 Birmingham, England

Polke, Sigmar

Second Netherlands Journey, 1985

'Sigmar Polke is a brilliantly witty artist', writes British novelist A. S. Byatt. She means that she finds him funny, but much more. 'I use the word "wit" in the way it was used of English 17th-century poetry, to describe a ranging and probing intelligence that investigates everything, connecting disparate images and ideas.'

Polke is loosely associated with the 1980s school known as Neo-Expressionism, another pendulum swing in art, this time back from elegance and chastity to raw emotion. Yet there is more to these works than feeling, impassioned as they often are: wit, in every sense of the word, plays an important part. Like Gerhard Richter (b. 1932), another artist often associated with Neo-Expressionism, Polke grew up in a nation that no longer exists, the German Democratic Republic. The people of this Soviet satellite state were always conscious of being only half a country, with West Germany sensed as a presence like an amputated limb. It gave East Germans a unique perspective on the culture of the Cold War. In the 1960s Polke and Richter took a cynical view of both ideological orders, developing their own irreverent Pop Art, 'Capitalist Realism'.

CREATED

Cologne

MEDIUM

Mixed media and lacquer on furnishing fabric

PERIOD/SERIES/MOVEMENT

Neo-Expressionism

SIMILAR WORKS

Gerhard Richter, *Abstract Painting, 780-1*, 1992

Anselm Kiefer, *Bohemia Lies by the Sea*, 1996

Sigmar Polke *Born* 1941 Olesnicka, Germany

Kossoff, Leon

Here Comes the Diesel, 1987

Courtesy of Private Collection/www.bridgeman.co.uk/© Leon Kossoff

The so-called School of London, as has been the way with many such 'movements' in modern art, was really no more than a loose assemblage of broadly like-minded artists. Its origins go back to the 1940s and the work of Francis Bacon (1909–92) and Lucian Freud (b. 1922), and many members since have shared their fascination with the form and beauty of the human body, although this was never their exclusive subject, as the painting here makes clear.

There was never any rigid agenda and the 'school' has embodied as many aesthetic philosophies as it has had members, but the general tendency has been broadly 'Expressionist'. Leon Kossoff is typical of the school in being a strongly independent-minded individualist, but also in producing deeply felt and visually hard-hitting images. Here an everyday scene is endowed with an almost shocking intensity: the thick impasto seems to have been laid on with a trowel. The sheer mass of solidified paint, paradoxically, gives an effect of liquid instability: the yellow front of the locomotive seems afloat at the centre of a seething cauldron of colour, dark and menacing.

CREATED

London

MEDIUM

Oil on board

PERIOD/SERIES/MOVEMENT

School of London/Neo-Expressionism

SIMILAR WORKS

Howard Hodgkin, *Rain*, 1984–89

Frank Auerbach, *To the Studios*, 1990

Leon Kossoff *Born* 1926 London, England

Patterson, Simon

The Great Bear, 1992

Like Marcus Harvey's *Myra*, this work gives an iconic image a contemporary makeover — this time, however, the less sinister one of the London Underground map. Harry Beck's original of 1933 is a design classic: taking its inspiration from the idea of the electrical circuit diagram, it envisioned Britain's capital as a throbbing centre of social, commercial and political energy.

As re-imagined by Patterson, the map becomes a constellation of stars, each station renamed after some celebrity, present or past. Artists, actors, philosophers, footballers and scientists have their own allotted lines. They criss-cross on the map as their influence does in contemporary culture. Hence Oxford Circus is Titian, from where you can take the Bakerloo line north, to Albert Einstein; or take the Victoria Line to footballer Gary Lineker and beyond. Leicester Square becomes an appropriately theatrical Sir Laurence Olivier; Euston Square is Karl Marx, and Euston, Zeppo Marx.

CREATED

London

MEDIUM & DIMENSIONS

Colour lithograph, 109.25 cm × 134.6 cm, Edition of 50

PERIOD/SERIES/MOVEMENT

Britart/Conceptual Art

SIMILAR WORKS

Gillian Wearing, *Signs that Say What You Want them to Say and Not Signs that Say What Someone Else Wants You to Say*, 1992–93

Gary Hume, *Snowman*, 1996

Simon Patterson *Born* 1967 Leatherhead, England

The Great Bear

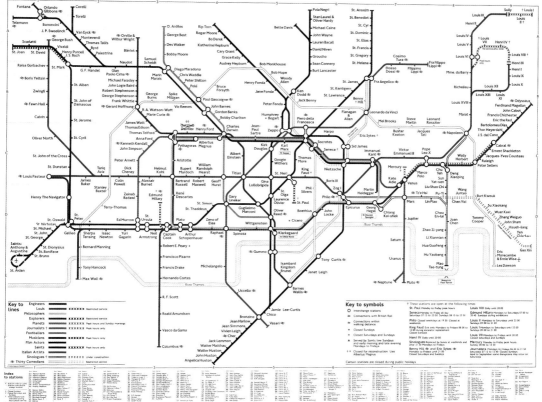

Modern Art

Portrait

Derain, André

Self Portrait with a Cap, c. 1905

André Derain was a friend of Henri Matisse, and had for a time shared a studio with Maurice de Vlaminck, so it was inevitable that he should have been one of the founding Fauves. A work like this one reminds us that, however 'wild' their palette and however untamed their technique, the Fauves were amiability itself in their relationship with their viewer, and never interested in attacking anything other than worn out convention.

With all its superficial outlandishness, this self-portrait is a work of genuine psychological depth: there is real warmth and intelligence in the expression of the artist-subject. Yet Derain does not assault us emotionally in the way the Expressionists would do: the impression we have is of a man at ease with himself and with his world. And, for that matter, with his art: this is a wonderfully accomplished work – eccentric in its parts, perhaps, but utterly convincing as a whole. The counterpointing of outline and surface texture, the play of contrasting colours, of shadow and sun, add up to an extraordinarily fresh and yet endlessly absorbing work of art.

CREATED

Paris

MEDIUM

Oil on canvas

PERIOD/SERIES/MOVEMENT

Fauvism

SIMILAR WORKS

Georges Rouault, *Nude with Raised Arm*, 1906

André Derain *Born* 1880 near Paris, France

Died 1954

Nolde, Emil

Prophet, 1912

'Conscientious and exact imitation of nature does not create a work of art. A wax figure confoundingly lifelike causes nothing but disgust. A work becomes a work of art when one re-evaluates the values of nature and adds one's own spirituality.'

Pioneer Expressionist Emil Nolde dedicated himself to the creation of deeply spiritual works, often, as here, with explicitly religious subjects. His concern was not to delineate in realist terms how any scriptural character or event might have immediately appeared, but to express the powerful emotions he felt were embodied in their stories. Captured in what at first appears to be the crudest of woodcuts, this prophet speaks eloquently, if ultimately to no avail. The massive flatness of the face suggests the solidity of the stone tablets of the law; the rugged features proclaim the majesty of God's word. The eyes, however, hold the anguish of the prophet 'dishonoured in his own country': his message of truth, he knows, was destined to be ignored by an impious age. Those younger artists who emulated Nolde did not necessarily share his religious convictions, but his profound intensity still struck a powerful chord.

CREATED

Berlin

MEDIUM & DIMENSIONS

Woodcut, 32.5 x 22 cm

PERIOD/SERIES/MOVEMENT

Expressionism

SIMILAR WORKS

Franz Marc, *The Bewitched Mill*, 1913

Emil Nolde (born Emil Hansen) *Born* 1867 Schleswig-Holstein, Germany

Died 1956

Kokoschka, Oskar

Adolf Loos, 1909

The truly artistic perception, suggested Kokoschka, 'derives its power from within itself'. Its 'free visualising', he said, 'has its own power running through. The effect is such that the visions seem actually to modify one's consciousness ... At the same time there is an outpouring of feeling into the image which becomes, as it were, the soul's plastic embodiment'. Kokoschka's artistic theorizing could be as impossibly abstruse as his actual creations were immediately arresting, but this one is worth teasing out a little. It highlights the central ambiguity in Kokoschka's famous 'psychological portraits': namely, whose psychology exactly do they portray? The popular conclusion is that they represent the 'inner life' of their subjects, but should they rather be seen as the 'plastic embodiment' of Kokoschka's own soul?

A century later it hardly matters whether the tensions that make such a coiled spring of architect Adolf Loos are those of the sitter himself or of Kokoschka. As we saw with Nolde's *Prophet*, the physical appearance of the individual is little more than the vehicle by which a more universal, more profound emotion is expressed.

CREATED

Vienna

MEDIUM

Oil on canvas

PERIOD/SERIES/MOVEMENT

Expressionism

SIMILAR WORKS

Erich Heckel, *Girl with Doll*, 1910

Oskar Kokoschka *Born* 1886 Pochlärn, Austria

Died 1980

Modersohn-Becker, Paula
Mother and Child, 1903

Paula Becker was first formed creatively by her time at Worpswede, an artists' colony outside Bremen, from 1898, and by her marriage there to fellow artist Otto Modersohn. The resulting painter was well-behaved, creating conservative – even rather sentimental – landscapes and portraits; appealing enough, but never the least bit surprising, still less unsettling. All this was to change, partly in response to the works of Vincent Van Gogh (1853–90) and Paul Gauguin (1848–1903) seen during a series of visits to Paris at the start of the century, and partly through her conversations with poet Rainer Maria Rilke (1875–1926), whose muse she became. Mostly, however, the breakthrough was her own resolution that she would hold fast to her 'personal vision'. Emotional integrity was at the centre of her work.

Determination is as much a feature of the mother here as it seems to have been of Paula: maternal love is matter of fact, and as tough as it is tender. No ethereal Madonna, this woman is a figure of physical strength and fierce protectiveness, but she still suggests a certain serenity and contentment. Tragically, the artist herself died in the aftermath of childbirth.

CREATED
Worpswede, near Bremen, Germany

MEDIUM
Oil on canvas

PERIOD/SERIES/MOVEMENT
Expressionism

SIMILAR WORKS
Alexei Jawlensky, *Head*, c. 1910

Paula Modersohn-Becker *Born* 1876 Dresden, Germany
Died 1907

Schiele, Egon
Seated Woman With Bent Knee, 1917

Despite being, in his own words, 'a nice young man from a respectable middle-class family', Egon Schiele spent just over three weeks in prison in 1912, convicted of offences against morality. Outraged at his work, his accusers failed to make the case that Schiele had molested any of his under-age models, and the only assault was against the bourgeois pieties. The Viennese mores of that time were notoriously hypocritical, of course, and Schiele's own attitudes to women and sex were profoundly ambivalent. He created sought-after society portraits, but at the same time many of his drawings did circulate as 'dirty pictures'.

The art criticism of recent years has, by and large, been severe on pornography and impatient of attempts to propose a respectable subcategory of 'erotica', seeing both as at best objectifying women, at worst misogynistic. Schiele is arguably guilty on both counts: their gazes indifferent, even impersonal, his twisted figures associate sex with destructiveness; they are contorted, not in pleasure, but in the agonies of death. So unsettling, however, is even a comparatively demure figure, such as this one, that his art seems to transcend all questions of 'political correctness'.

CREATED

Vienna

MEDIUM

Gouache, watercolour and black crayon on paper

PERIOD/SERIES/MOVEMENT

Expressionism

SIMILAR WORKS

Gustav Klimt, *Reclining Woman*, c. 1901–02

Egon Schiele *Born* 1890 Tulln, Austria

Died 1918

Heckel, Erich

White Circus Horse, 1921

Through the years of the First World War, Erich Heckel painted works of terrifying intensity: the sufferings of so many found expression in his work. For an artist already apt to see existence in terms of agony and injustice, the conflict convulsing Europe must have struck a profound psychological chord as a vast bloody metaphor come true.

Thereafter, Heckel's art changed — the colours softening, the mood apparently lightening, but we should not necessarily assume that Heckel himself had mellowed, as some critics have implied. In this circus scene from 1921, although we certainly see a festive subject done in pastel shades, we also find more than a suggestion of the grotesque. The immediate impression is of a scene less cheerful than it should be: the constricting circles in which the horse is condemned to run suggest a cramped and pointless existence. Acrobats are directed in improbable contortions by the gaunt figure of the top-hatted ringmaster with his whip, as a distinctly sinister clown surveys the audience. Is it fanciful to see a hint of social satire in this scene: a bridge, even, between *Die Brücke* and the *Neue Sachlichkeit*?

CREATED

Berlin

MEDIUM

Oil on canvas

PERIOD/SERIES/MOVEMENT

Die Brücke/Expressionism

SIMILAR WORKS

Max Beckmann, *Self-Portrait in Front of Red Curtain*, 1923

Erich Heckel *Born* 1883 Saxony, Germany, 1883

Died 1970

Bellows, George Wesley
Paddy Flannigan, 1905

New York Realism famously represents an early commitment to Realism in twentieth-century American art, but as the school's own output shows, there is 'realism' and 'realism'. Robert Henri's (1865–1929) *The Irish Girl* (c. 1900), for example, is unmistakeably realist in its approach, but his laughing-eyed colleen is, quite simply, 'as pretty as a picture'. Poor and down-to-earth she may be, but the drabness of her surroundings only frames her beauty and sweet nature. This work shows a world that is fundamentally benign. Just a few years away, but an artistic generation apart, George Wesley Bellows was staring wide-eyed at another world entirely, and finding horror where others had found picturesque appeal. Take his famous boxing scenes, for example: of *Stag at Sharkey's* (1909) Bellows observed, 'I don't know anything about boxing; I'm just painting two men trying to kill one another'. A joke, of course, but Bellows was being more serious than he sounded: his works depict a gloves-off existence, even by the standards of New York Realism. Made on a tour to Ireland, this portrait is a case in point, as there is nothing remotely attractive about poverty as shown here.

CREATED

New York

MEDIUM

Oil on canvas

PERIOD/SERIES/MOVEMENT

New York Realism/Ashcan School

SIMILAR WORKS

Robert Henri, *The Irish Girl*, c. 1900

George Wesley Bellows *Born* 1882 Columbus, OH, USA

Died 1925

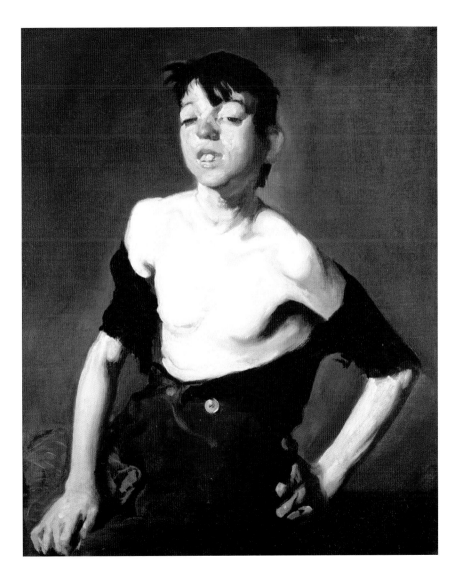

Sloan, John

Red Kimono on the Roof, 1912

Courtesy of Indianapolis Museum of Art, USA, James E. Roberts Fund/www.bridgeman.co.uk/© Estate of John Sloan

Like several other New York Realist painters, including school founders such as William Glackens (1870–1938), George Benjamin Luks (1866–1933) and Everett Shinn (1876–1953), Sloan had been an illustrator for the press before he became a full-time painter. Drawings in late-nineteenth century magazines and newspapers performed the function that photographs do today, giving a sense of the drama and human interest in the news. As with news photos today, they did not concern themselves only with great events, but dealt too with quirkier items of curiosity and human interest.

Altogether, news illustration was underpinned by an aesthetic of the everyday, disposed to find interest and colour in apparently mundane events and existences. So it was with the artists of the Ashcan School: theirs was not necessarily an ideologically driven 'social' realism, nor could it for the most part be seen as being seriously documentary in its purpose. However, it was genuinely democratic in its interest in the experiences of ordinary people. This is clearly to be seen in the picture shown here, as is a delight in the events of the fleeting moment , which lends a certain proto-photographic character.

CREATED

New York

MEDIUM

Oil on canvas

PERIOD/SERIES/MOVEMENT

New York Realism/Ashcan School

SIMILAR WORKS

George Benjamin Luks, *In the Steerage*, 1900

John Sloan *Born* 1871 Lock Haven, PA, USA

Died 1951

Picasso, Pablo

Les Demoiselles d'Avignon, 1907

The French title suggests a stiff and formal tableau of stately, perhaps medieval figures, but Picasso had another Avignon and other *demoiselles* in mind. His setting was Avignon Street, notorious as the centre of Barcelona's early twentieth-century red light district; his ladies were, accordingly, young whores. The fruit in the foreground is forbidden, then, and the women almost seem to be daring the viewer to taste it. Critical writings on Cubist theory may suggest an over-analytic, even diagrammatic style of a sort never to be convincingly realized in living, human art. Slavish adherence to Cubist principles could produce works of intellectualized sterility, no doubt, but the movement's founders, Georges Braque (1882–1963) and Picasso, were striving for more vividness, not less. It helped having their talent, of course: Picasso's in particular was truly prodigious. He shows here not only how the Cubist project could come alive, but also why he is regarded as the single greatest artist of the twentieth century. He worked in every field from painting and drawing to sculpture and ceramics, revolutionizing just about all. He was nothing less than a one-man Modernist renaissance.

CREATED

Paris

MEDIUM

Oil on canvas

PERIOD/SERIES/MOVEMENT

Cubism

SIMILAR WORKS

Marcel Duchamp, *Nude Descending a Staircase, No. 2*, 1912

Pablo Picasso *Born* 1881 Málaga, Spain

Died 1973

Léger, Fernand
The Pilot, 1920

Having been a draughtsman in an architects' practice, Fernand Léger took up painting around 1900, and from 1909 he became an enthusiastic but unorthodox Cubist. His earlier apprenticeship perhaps informed his interest in geometrical structures, which became increasingly prominent in his work. By the time he painted this one, it was teetering on the very brink of abstraction, yet this is still just about recognizable as representational work. Characteristically it gives us a sense not only of the pilot, but also of his aeroplane, with its propeller, its controls and internal workings. Léger's fascination with all things mechanical echoes that of the Italian Futurists and leads to similarities between their works, but his interest was altogether different. In his lecture, published in 1924, 'The Aesthetic of the Machine', he makes it clear that the appeal of technology lies not in its power and ferocity, but in the fact that it belongs to the domain of the everyday into which aesthetics has not hitherto ventured much. 'Beauty is everywhere,' he says, 'in the arrangement of your pots and pans, on the white wall of your kitchen, more perhaps than in your eighteenth-century salon or in the official museum.'

CREATED

Paris

MEDIUM

Oil on canvas

PERIOD/SERIES/MOVEMENT

Cubism

SIMILAR WORKS

Albert Gleizes, *Portrait of a Young Man*, c. 1910

Fernand Léger *Born* 1881 Argentan, France

Died 1955

Macke, August

Woman in a Green Jacket, 1913

© Ludwig Museum, Cologne, Germany/www.bridgeman.co.uk

'Incomprehensible ideas have comprehensible forms ...', wrote August Macke in 1912 in a contribution to the almanac of the *Der Blaue Reiter* movement. 'The senses are our bridge between the incomprehensible and the comprehensible...', he continued: 'Forms are powerful expressions of powerful life.' Or so, at least they should be: Macke went on to deplore the divorce between increasingly empty, prettified forms in western art, and the deep emotional wellsprings of human life. He professed himself astonished, as well as disgusted, at the banishment of 'primitive' art to the ethnographical museum. European artists should recover the savage's connection with the elemental, he insisted.

Twentieth-century art was never to be short of such radical rallying cries, of course, and often the bigger the declaration the smaller the achievement. Yet there is no disputing the fact that Macke was accessing profound emotions in his art, and doing so, as he claimed, through works of immense simplicity. Despite his rhetoric he created some of German Expressionism's least portentous works: it is no surprise to find that he was greatly influenced by French models, such as the paintings of the Fauves.

CREATED

Munich

MEDIUM

Oil on canvas

PERIOD/SERIES/MOVEMENT

Der Blaue Reiter/Expressionism

SIMILAR WORKS

Alexei von Jawlensky, *Seated Woman*, 1911

August Macke *Born* 1887 Westphalia, Germany

Died 1914

Marc, Franz

Spingende Pferd ('Wheeling Horse'), 1913

'How does a horse see the world?' asked Franz Marc in 1920. He was haunted by the idea that there were potentially limitless ways of perceiving existence; the challenge for the human artist was not simply to articulate his own perspective but to explore alternative possibilities. 'It is a poverty-stricken convention to place animals in landscapes as seen by men; instead, we should contemplate the soul of the animal to divine its way of sight.' How successfully he has done so here in *Wheeling Horse* is open to debate; a debate that could of course never conceivably be resolved without the animal's authoritative testimony. Yet he does manage to suggest such inherently elusive qualities as instinctual feeling, speed and strength. Marc, a co-founder of *Der Blaue Reiter*, devoted more and more of his attentions to animals in art as time went on, finding in them a spirituality he felt was not discernible in his fellow men and women. As with Oskar Kokoschka's (1886–1980) 'psychological portraits', with which they are arguably analogous, these works tell us much more about the artist's psychology than that of their supposed subjects', but they are not diminished artistically by that fact.

CREATED

Munich

MEDIUM

Oil on canvas

PERIOD/SERIES/MOVEMENT

Der Blaue Reiter / Expressionism

SIMILAR WORKS

Gabriele Münter, *Still Life with St George*, 1911

Franz Marc *Born* 1880 Munich, Germany

Died 1916

Wyndham Lewis, Percy

Alcibiades, from the *Timon of Athens* portfolio, 1912

Alcibiades, the Athenian statesman who, having been ostracized and sent into banishment as a traitor, returned as conqueror to his homeland, made the perfect subject for Wyndham Lewis. He had chosen the course of exile for himself, but it was in keeping with his own heroic self-image that he should regard his years in Paris as the price of a genius reared among Philistines. As for the triumphant return, this too would arguably be achieved, although it took some years for it to be brought about. Fortunately Wyndham Lewis was a tireless self-publicist, a writer as well as an artist of real originality, and he marshalled influential supporters such as the poets T. S. Eliot and Ezra Pound. This work was informed by Cubism, and predates the full-blown Vorticism by which he would win fame. 'At the heart of a whirlpool is a great silent place where all the energy is concentrated ...' Wyndham Lewis wrote, 'and there ... is The Vorticist.' The choice of natural image, the 'whirlpool', rather than the mechanistic monsters favoured by the Futurists, obscures the underlying similarities between their works.

CREATED

London

MEDIUM

Pen and ink wash on paper

PERIOD/SERIES/MOVEMENT

Futurism/Vorticism

SIMILAR WORKS

Henri Gaudier-Brzeska, *The Wrestlers*, Marquetry Tray, 1913

Percy Wyndham Lewis *Born* 1882 Nova Scotia, Canada

Died 1957

Heartfield, John

The Political Conference of the SPD in Crisis, 1931

Courtesy of Private Collection/www.bridgeman.co.uk/© The Heartfield Community of Heirs/VG Bild-Kunst, Bonn & DACS, London 2005

Dada's delight in the illogical and the absurd did not mean that it took no interest in contemporary realities – often the nonsensical was an important element in current affairs. John Heartfield was certainly no artistic buffoon, however outlandish his imagery. He was the son of a famous socialist radical, and a committed reformer in his own right. In 1930 he began an association with the leftist newspaper *Arbeiter Illustrierte Zeitung* (*AIZ*, 'Workers' Illustrated News'), which would go on for eight years and prove profoundly stimulating for his work. The Dadaist interest in 'readymade' components was already well developed, and printed materials were already being mined for images: now it could become a two-way process. Heartfield's withering visual satires on Hitler and his Nazis would eventually see the *AIZ* shut down and Heartfield forced into exile. This forceful photomontage derides the faint-hearted philosophy of the German SPD (Social Democratic Party), which wished to ease the sufferings of the poor without changing the capitalist system. They wanted, in Heartfield's scathing view, to draw the tiger's teeth while keeping the beast itself alive and well.

CREATED

Berlin

MEDIUM

Photomontage

PERIOD/SERIES/MOVEMENT

Dada

SIMILAR WORKS

Raoul Hausmann, *The Art Critic*, 1919–20

John Heartfield (born Helmut Herzfelde) *Born* 1891 Berlin, Germany

Died 1968

ZUM KRISENPARTEITAG DER S.P.D.

Richter, Hans

Dada Kopf ('Dada Head'), 1918

Hans Richter took himself to Zurich in 1916 after being invalided out of the German Army during the First World War, one of several artistic refugees to find sanctuary in the capital of neutral Switzerland. Another of their number, Jean Arp (1886–1966) described Dada as growing out of that gathering of talents, and their desire to find artistic escape from the apocalypse that was taking place around them: 'In Zurich in 1915, losing interest in the slaughterhouses of the world war, we turned to the Fine Arts. With the thunder of the batteries in the distance, we pasted, we recited, we versified, we sang with our soul. We searched for an elementary art that would, we thought, save mankind from the furious folly of these times.'

There was, then, a certain degree of method in the madness of the Dadaists, a reaction against what they saw as the monstrous insanity of a world in arms. Rationalism, Realism and other 'bourgeois' conventions had brought humanity only to intellectual and moral bankruptcy, they felt: it was time now for nonsense to inherit the earth.

CREATED

Zurich

MEDIUM

Gouache on canvas

PERIOD/SERIES/MOVEMENT

Dada

SIMILAR WORKS

Jean Arp, *Two Heads*, 1927

Hans Richter *Born* 1888 Berlin, Germany

Died 1976

van der Leck, Bart

Woman and Cow, 1922

Courtesy of Christie's Images Ltd/© DACS 2005

With its clean, uncluttered lines and simple geometric shapes, all represented in the purest and boldest of colours, the art of *De Stijl* exudes modernity and clarity of conception. It comes as quite a shock, therefore, to find that it is rooted in mysticism, but its most famous practitioner, Piet Mondrian, was in no doubt. A 'Neo-Plasticist' art would seek out the true plasticity (or reality), he said; this meant shunning the false plasticity of the particular. The individuating detail, the irregular shape, the shade of colour: all these existed in opposition to the real reality, the absolute, the universal. Externality and the interior being were similarly opposed. The former, although not to be despised, was insufficient in itself and an inadequate object of study for the artist: the challenge was to find a balance between the two. Such equilibrium might be replicated in interior design, and even in architecture and town planning: *De Stijl* offered a vision of Utopia.

Van der Leck eventually moved away from doctrinaire 'Neo-Plasticism' of this sort, but he remained true to its aesthetic values, as we see here.

CREATED

Amsterdam

MEDIUM

Lithograph, after 1921 painting

PERIOD/SERIES/MOVEMENT

De Stijl/Neo-Plasticism

SIMILAR WORKS

Theo van Doesburg, *Composition (The Cow)*, c. 1917

Bart van der Leck *Born* 1876 Utrecht, Netherlands

Died 1958

BvoLeck

Klee, Paul
The Lamb, 1920

In the same year in which he created this animal figure, Paul Klee published his *Creative Credo*: 'Art does not reproduce the visible; rather, it makes visible', it said. 'A tendency towards the abstract is inherent in linear expression: graphic imagery being confined to outlines has a fairy-like quality and at the same time can achieve great precision.'

A work such as this one evidently exploits this twofold quality, representational form and abstract background each counterpointing and complementing one another. Colour is counterpointed too: by early training as an etching specialist, Klee had come to colour relatively late in his artistic development. He sensed its importance in the works of his friend and mentor Wassily Kandinsky (1886–1944), and in 1910 recorded his ambition to be able to improvise freely on the 'keyboard of adjacent pots of paint'. The breakthrough came in the sunshine of Tunisia, where he went with August Macke and Louis Moilliet in 1914. 'Colour has got me', he wrote. 'I don't need to run after it. It's got me forever, I know it. That is the meaning of this happy hour: colour and I are one. I am a painter.'

CREATED

Munich

MEDIUM

Watercolour

PERIOD/SERIES/MOVEMENT

Der Blaue Reiter/Expressionism

SIMILAR WORKS

Franz Marc, *Tiger*, 1912

Paul Klee *Born* 1879 Munchenbuchsee, Switzerland

Died 1940

de Lempicka, Tamara
Nude with Buildings, 1930

Courtesy of NYC Christie's Images Ltd/© ADAGP, Paris & DACS, London 2005

Art Deco took its name from the *Exposition Internationale des Arts Décoratifs et Industriels Modernes*, which was staged in Paris in 1925. It was a style of overall design, within which painting had to take its place as just one creative discipline among many, as everything from architecture to automobiles was encompassed. Lacquered lamps, ebony cigarette holders, cocktail glasses of sparkling crystal: Art Deco was closely (and unabashedly) associated with wealth and glamour. However, its interest in the trappings of wealth meant that it was associated with the consumerist end of modern technology too: fast cars, express trains, airliners, telephones. An obsession with streamlining crept in, and 'trickled down' the social scale, influencing such comparatively humble and entirely static consumer goods as cookers and refrigerators.

So, although it was drawn towards such things by a mild-mannered social snobbery rather than an aggressive proto-Fascism, Art Deco ended up sharing certain preoccupations with Futurism. Here, then, Lempicka's statuesque nude is set against a background of stylized skyscraper buildings: phallic to be sure, but, more important, modern.

CREATED

Paris

MEDIUM

Oil on canvas

PERIOD/SERIES/MOVEMENT

Art Deco

SIMILAR WORKS

A. M. Cassandre, *L'Oiseau Bleu* (Bluebird, Pullman poster), 1929

Tamara de Lempicka (born Tamara Gorska) *Born* 1898 Warsaw, Poland

Died 1980

Burra, Edward

Salome

Edward Burra's work defies categorization in terms of artistic 'movement': like L. S. Lowry (1887–1976) and Stanley Spencer (1891–1959), he belongs to the 'English Eccentrics' school. Like them, however, he was more a man of the artistic world than is often imagined: he had trained at London's Royal Academy, travelled widely in Europe and North America, and soaked up all the influences of modern art, especially those of Surrealism and Dada. So much is evident in this painting of a saloon-bar Salome in avian form, wheeling away behind her hard-won head of John the Baptist, which is displayed on a table before a cast of animal characters that might have come from a children's story. Also apparent is the influence of Germany's George Grosz, whom Burra avowedly admired, although his world view was for the most part more indulgent. Burra's brothels and drinking dives generally seem symbolically self-contained: we do not have the sense we do in Grosz's works that they are microcosms of a decadent society. Not until 1936, with the Spanish Civil War, do we see his mood significantly darkening, English good humour being no longer adequate in the face of a tragic slaughter.

CREATED

London

MEDIUM

Watercolour

PERIOD/SERIES/MOVEMENT

Surrealism

SIMILAR WORKS

George Grosz, *The Pillars of Society*, 1926

Edward Burra *Born* 1905 London, England

Died 1976

Chagall, Marc

A Midsummer Night's Dream, 1939

Tiny fairies fly around as Bottom the weaver embraces their Queen, Titania, in Chagall's vision of Shakespeare's *A Midsummer Night's Dream*. The worlds of magic, fantasy and the unreal were spheres in which the Russian-Jewish artist felt very much at home, steeped in the spirituality of his race and in the folklore of his homeland as he was.

He was encouraged in both by Léon Bakst (1866–1924), under whom he studied in St Petersburg for a while before heading west to enrol in the *École de Paris*. All the main movements, from Cubism to Orphism, had an impact on his work, but Chagall persevered until he had developed a style all his own. Deceptively naïve, it tends towards a religious luminosity (Chagall experimented with stained-glass work), but with none of the ecclesiastical solemnity that may seem to imply. His work is often playful and fanciful, but its charming fairy-tale quality should not blind us to the fact that it often dealt seriously with the great tragedies of existence. Although as good-humoured in art as he was in life, Chagall was a deeply serious artist and one of the most important of his time.

CREATED

Munich

MEDIUM

Oil on canvas

PERIOD/SERIES/MOVEMENT

École de Paris

SIMILAR WORKS

Léon Bakst, *Set Design for the Ballet Schéhérazade*, 1910

Marc Chagall *Born* 1887 Vitebsk, Russia

Died 1985

Modigliani, Amedeo

Portrait of Madame Hanka Zborowska, 1917

So striking is this portrait that the viewer hardly notices quite how improbable, even grotesque, it is, such is the surpassing magic of Modigliani. The extravagant white collar only draws attention to the exaggeratedly shapely neck it seems to frame, and the drawing-manual features to be seen above. The nose, at once dainty and elongated, is set off by exquisite eyebrows that arc over the mismatched eyes: the single irregularity, which gives life to the whole portrait. The result, although almost stylized in form, is irresistibly lifelike in its effect: we see not just a beautiful face, but a lively, thinking, feeling woman.

Modigliani's female figures have often been compared with Botticelli's: he certainly appears to have studied the Renaissance art of his native Italy before he left for Paris. Arriving there in 1906, he threw himself into the Bohemian life. In 1909, prompted by his sculptor friend Constantin Brancusi (1876–1957) he formed the little circle, *Les Maudits*, along with Chaim Soutine (1893–1943), Maurice Utrillo (1883–1955) and Jules Pascin (1885–1930). Modigliani was indeed accursed, afflicted by tuberculosis, alcoholism and drug addiction, but his work seems serenely untroubled by such cares.

CREATED

Paris

MEDIUM

Oil on canvas

PERIOD/SERIES/MOVEMENT

École de Paris

SIMILAR WORKS

Jules Pascin, *La Mélancolique*, 1909

Amedeo Modigliani *Born* 1884 Livorno, Italy

Died 1920

Shahn, Ben

Unemployment, 1938

Raised in a Brooklyn slum, Ben Shahn's political activist parents had been among the many thousands of the Tsar's subjects seeking sanctuary in the United States of America at the start of the century. Shahn accordingly grew up not only with a deep commitment to social justice, but with a cosmopolitan context in which to view American life. The trial of Nicola Sacco and Bartolomeo Vanzetti in 1921 marked his coming of age both as artist and radical, and he kept a celebrated picture record of proceedings. The two Italian anarchists were in theory arraigned and executed for a murder committed in the course of an armed robbery, but it was always clear that this was a political trial.

Shahn naturally gravitated to Communism, and what amounted to an artist's international group in which Diego Rivera was the leading figure. The New Yorker assisted the Mexican muralist when in 1932–34 he created his great *Man at the Crossroads* mural at the Rockefeller Center. Rivera was paid off and his painting destroyed when the oil tycoon took exception to the presence of Lenin at the centre of the picture. It was subsequently recreated in Mexico City.

CREATED

New York

MEDIUM

Tempera on paper

PERIOD/SERIES/MOVEMENT

Social Realism

SIMILAR WORKS

Reginald Marsh, *10th Avenue Street Corner*, 1931

Ben Shahn *Born* 1898 Kovno, Lithuania

Died 1969

Dubuffet, Jean
Antonin Artaud, 1950

The notion that genius is akin to insanity is as old as it is dubious: perhaps inevitably it exercised an appeal on the Surrealists. Not until the postwar period, however, did the French artist and critic Jean Dubuffet set out to build an artistic movement around the work of society's outcasts.

Art Brut ('Raw Art'), as he called it, would model itself on the work of the mentally ill and other marginalized figures, whom Dubuffet saw as not 'lacking in' but being free of formal training. Likewise their stylistic naïvety, far from representing a handicap, marked a liberation from conventional constraints. How convincing one finds this theory really depends on how disposed one is to be convinced, and Dubuffet's claims prompt as many questions as they do answers. How, for instance, is the 'sane' artist to achieve the freedom he supposes the mad to possess? And what is the artistic advantage should he or she succeed? The evidence of artists such as Adolf Wölfli (a Dubuffet protégé) suggests that such people may be 'locked into' their own obsessions just as surely as they are confined by their hospital wards.

CREATED

Paris

MEDIUM

Oil on canvas

PERIOD/SERIES/MOVEMENT

Art Brut/'Outsider Art'

SIMILAR WORKS

Adolf Wölfli, *H.M. Queen Hortensia on the Telephone*, 1920

Jean Dubuffet *Born* 1901 Le Havre, France

Died 1985

Bacon, Francis
Head VI, 1949

Velasquez, Bacon suggested, really believed he was recording the court of his time; however, photography and philosophy had put paid to that idea between them. Offering accurate representations instantaneously, the former had usurped the artist's role as chronicler of unfolding lives, while the latter had called into question the very nature of existence. The artist, Bacon concluded, could no longer delude himself that he was fixing any sort of reality; art, he said, had become 'a game by which man distracts himself'. It was thus its own inspiration and provided its own motive and force: every painting was an 'accident', he believed. The very application of the paint transformed the conception of the work as it went along, with the finished painting representing its own reality. Hence, the head shown here has its own artistic integrity, although clearly incomplete from a conventionally realistic point of view. Along with Lucian Freud (b. 1922), Leon Kossoff (b. 1926), Frank Auerbach (b. 1931) and others, Bacon belonged to what became known as the School of London. This was a more-than-usually arbitrary designation, for while Bacon was a social animal – even a hell-raiser – artistically he walked alone.

CREATED

London

MEDIUM

Oil on canvas

PERIOD/SERIES/MOVEMENT

Existential Art/School of London

SIMILAR WORKS

Graham Sutherland, *Thorn Head*, 1946

Francis Bacon *Born* 1909 Dublin, Ireland

Died 1992

Freud, Lucian
Head of a Boy, 1954

Courtesy of Private Collection/www.bridgeman.co.uk/© Lucian Freud

From the point of view of technique, this could be seen as a Realist – even Superrealist – portrait, but there is an 'in-your-face' quality about this particular face that disconcerts. Utterly conventional in apparent essentials, it is nevertheless profoundly and unaccountably unsettling, and that is the Freud effect in a nutshell. It had been so ever since he made his artistic breakthrough in 1951 with *Interior at Paddington* (now in the Walker Art Gallery, Liverpool) and has continued to be so to this day. A certain washed-out pallor contributes to the effect in this painting, as does the subtly lopsided impression given by the nose and upper lip. More important, perhaps, is the slightly shifty way in which the subject avoids our gaze: this is a work that, albeit very quietly, breaks the rules.

Like his friend Francis Bacon, Lucian Freud is associated with the School of London, although once again the label tells us little about his work. His German-Jewish father, Ernst, an architect and son of the founder of psychoanalysis, Sigmund Freud, brought Lucian to England in 1932 when he was still a boy.

CREATED

London

MEDIUM

Oil on canvas

PERIOD/SERIES/MOVEMENT

Existential Art/School of London

SIMILAR WORKS

Michael Andrews, *Study of a Man in a Landscape (Digswell)*, 1959

Leon Kossoff, *Leon Kossoff*, 1981

Lucian Freud *Born* 1922 Berlin, Germany

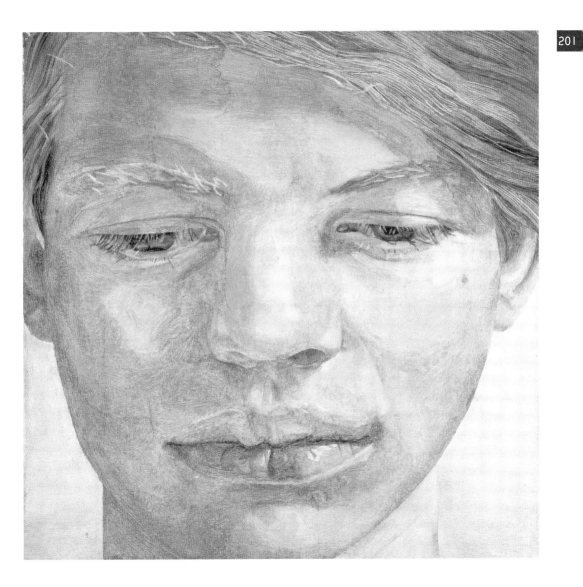

de Kooning, Willem
Marilyn Monroe, 1954

Willem de Kooning's Abstract Expressionism was not necessarily completely abstract, although the film star has been swept up into an emotion greater and wilder than her own iconic image here. The precise nature of that emotion, and whether it is as a positive or negative one, is altogether harder to pin down.

An earlier series by De Kooning (*Woman I–VI*, 1950–52) had already incurred the wrath of doctrinaire critics who felt that the figurative age in art had gone. It was subsequently to attract criticism from feminist critics, too. Taken to extremes (as occasionally it has been), the case against them was that these works represented their subjects as dehumanized puppets and, worse, that they were painted in such a violent flurry of ungoverned brushstrokes as to amount to the artistic equivalent of a frenzied knife attack. Such judgements are subjective, of course: if de Kooning's picture is indeed informed by a deep-seated misogyny, it still offers a revealing and disturbing insight into 1950s culture. In addition, however negative its passion, it offers a profound ironic contrast to the empty shell of celebrity that is paraded in Andy Warhol's (1928–87) Marilyn prints.

CREATED

New York

MEDIUM

Oil on canvas

PERIOD/SERIES/MOVEMENT

Abstract Expressionism

SIMILAR WORKS

Arshile Gorky, *Betrothal II*, 1947

Willem de Kooning *Born* 1904 Rotterdam, Netherlands

Died 1967

Appel, Karel
Child III, 1951

Courtesy of Haags Gemeentemuseum, The Hague, Netherlands/www.bridgeman.co.uk/© Karel Appel Foundation/DACS, London 2005

The CoBrA group comprised of artists drawn from Denmark, Belgium and the Netherlands, taking its name from the cities of Copenhagen, Brussels and Amsterdam. Postwar heirs to Expressionism, they saw themselves as being in revolt against what they saw as the empty geometric play of the abstract art being created in Europe at the time and the banality of the Socialist Realism, which seemed the only alternative on offer. They regarded themselves as revolutionaries, not just in the artistic but also in the political sense, although their project never seemed remotely practical. One spokesman, Constant (Constant Niewenhuys) called for the overthrow of pretty much everything that was established and familiar: 'When we say desire in the Twentieth Century, we mean the unknown.'

Their work was in some ways analogous to that of Art Brut: they sought to attain a powerful Primitivism that would enable them to bypass the conventions and find the deeper wellsprings of human feeling. Nordic mythology, modern folklore and prehistoric archaeology all influenced their work, but so too did other 'unofficial' forms such as graffiti and children's art.

CREATED

Paris

MEDIUM

Oil on canvas

PERIOD/SERIES/MOVEMENT

CoBrA

SIMILAR WORKS

Constant, *Lente* ('Spring'), 1949

Corneille, *Bord Fleuri d'une Rivière* ('Flowery Bank of a Stream'), 1955

Karel Appel *Born* 1921 Amsterdam, Netherlands

Kitaj, R. B.

Good News for Incunabulists, 1962

American-born Kitaj was the man who in 1976 first conjured into existence the School of London, and as the institution's founder was able to award himself a place. The only real similarity between his works and those of classmates such as Lucian Freud, Francis Bacon and Frank Auerbach was that, like them, he was a 'figurative' painter. His work really belongs in the early history of Pop Art – even in its prehistory, it might be said: Kitaj would never be entirely comfortable with the mass culture that Pop Art proper used. His commitment was always very obviously to a 'higher' art. Hence the apparent half-heartedness of a picture that appears to 'want' to be a photomontage, but is instead a work of old-fashioned draughtsmanship and painting.

If Britain could claim to have 'invented' Pop Art, American critics felt, not altogether unreasonably, a certain proprietorship over its imagery: they often felt they detected a certain stuffy fastidiousness in the way it was handled by British artists in the early days. Some examples, sneered Thomas Hess, not only looked impossibly 'bookish', but actually appeared to have been 'made by librarians'.

CREATED

London

MEDIUM

Oil on canvas

PERIOD/SERIES/MOVEMENT

Pop Art

SIMILAR WORKS

Allen Jones, *Hermaphrodite*, 1963

Patrick Caulfield, *Greece Expiring on the Ruins of Missolonghi (After Delacroix)*, 1963

Ron B. Kitaj *Born* 1932 Cleveland, OH, USA

Hockney, David

Cleanliness is Next to Godliness, 1964

Courtesy of Wolverhampton Art Gallery, West Midlands, UK/www.bridgeman.co.uk/© David Hockney

With its unalloyed pleasure in all things cheap and tacky, Pop Art is close kin to camp, the aesthetic of what by the 1960s was an increasingly confident gay subculture. In the course of that decade, homosexuality would be decriminalized in Britain and America, and 1969 would see New York's gay community come together for its own defence against official harassment in the 'Stonewall Riots'.

When the young David Hockney left a dreary, rainswept London for Los Angeles in 1963, he went in search not only of sunshine, but also of sex – and self-respect. Attitudes among urban sophisticates in California were far in advance of prevailing values elsewhere. Here it was possible to be a 'gay artist' true to self and sexuality, and with Pop Art fashionable there was a style ready-made. This witty little squib from 1964 shows an attractive hunk half-hidden in a shower, the curtain displaying his body even as it supposedly conceals. The title pokes mischievous fun at the sort of puritanism encapsulated in the old saying: the picture's purpose, of course, is anything but 'clean'.

CREATED

Los Angeles

MEDIUM

Screen print

PERIOD/SERIES/MOVEMENT

Pop Art

SIMILAR WORKS

Richard Hamilton, *Adonis in Y-Fronts*, 1962–63

Robert Indiana, *Sex Anyone?*, 1964

David Hockney *Born* 1937 Bradford, England

Tilson, Joe
Clip-o-Matic Lips, 1967

Film and the photographic media were long held to have rendered many of the functions of art redundant, but Pop Art was a way of co-opting them as a new set of artistic tools. There was much more to it than that, of course: Pop Art can now be seen to have anticipated the 'postmodern' preoccupation with the way the image is reproduced and propagated in contemporary media. Artists have often seen their task as the representation of representation itself: images of images-within-images have recurred in recent art.

Here we see seductive lips presented within the rectangular cell of a film frame, with previous and subsequent frames to be glimpsed on either side. The result is particularly interesting, revealing as it does a concern to explore the place of the image not just in its spatial dimensions but also in time. Classic art is stereotypically supposed to stand for uniqueness and timelessness, but Pop Art rejoices in the ephemeral and the endlessly reproducible: this picture shows a moment that, though fleeting, may be recaptured *ad infinitum*.

CREATED

London

MEDIUM

Photomontage

PERIOD/SERIES/MOVEMENT

Pop Art

SIMILAR WORKS

Andy Warhol, *Five Deaths Seventeen Times in Black and White*, 1963

Richard Hamilton, *Palindrome*, 1974

Joe Tilson *Born* 1928 London, England

Blake, Peter
Got a Girl, 1960–61

'Well I got a girl, what a girl/I don't know what to do./When she's with me, it's plain to see/There's someone else there too … There was Fabian, Avalon, Ricky Nelson,/Yeah, yeah, yeah, yeah,/Bobby Rydell and I know darned well, Presley's in there too.'

Peter Blake is perhaps best known today as the designer of the famous cover for the 1967 Beatles album *Sergeant Pepper's Lonely Hearts Club Band*. Yet his interest in pop music had begun long before, as had his sense that it was destined to impact upon the world of art, as shown in this extraordinary work created at the very beginning of the 1960s. Really it could be said to qualify as an early installation: it represents the locket of the girl in the Four Preps song, which opens as she embraces her boyfriend to send this incriminating stream of pop-star photographs spilling. The record displayed at top left was quite authentic: it could be taken out and played to provide an appropriate soundtrack to complete the experience, but which work was then the 'lead', and which the 'backing'?

CREATED

London

MEDIUM

Montage (oil, wood, photo collage and record on hardboard)

PERIOD/SERIES/MOVEMENT

Pop Art

SIMILAR WORKS

Andy Warhol, *Triple Elvis*, 1964

Richard Hamilton, *Swingeing London*, 1967

Peter Blake *Born* 1932 Dartford, England

Lichtenstein, Roy
Eddie Diptych, 1962

Since Pop Art took the imagery of mass culture as its subject, it was drawn irresistibly to the mass media by which that culture was transmitted. Many artists created stupendous works in montage, using ready-made images, but Roy Lichtenstein famously went further. Magnifying the frames of cheap strip cartoons to many times their original size, he fashioned them into works of art in the classic mould, painting in their Ben Day dots with loving detail through a special paper stencil.

In doing so he took the most stereotypical of images and the most hackneyed of sentiments and placed them on the pedestal previously reserved for the 'highest' art. Here, for example, in the drama of the jilted girl, he has created a 'diptych', a hinged two-panel painting of a sort associated with medieval religious art. This 'cod-canonification' undoubtedly brought out the banality of the strips that had inspired them, but Lichtenstein's purpose was certainly not to sneer. Indeed, he admired his models and aspired to replicate in conventional art the impersonal perfection he found in such mass-produced, industrially printed media, and in this respect he anticipated the Superrealists.

CREATED

New York

MEDIUM

Oil and acrylic

PERIOD/SERIES/MOVEMENT

Pop Art

SIMILAR WORKS

James Rosenquist, *World's Fair Mural*, 1963–64

Roy Lichtenstein *Born* 1923 New York, USA

Died 1997

I TRIED TO REASON IT OUT / I TRIED TO SEE THINGS FROM MOM AND DAD'S VIEW-POINT / I TRIED NOT TO THINK OF EDDIE, SO MY MIND WOULD BE CLEAR AND COMMON SENSE COULD TAKE OVER / BUT EDDIE KEPT COMING BACK...

Close, Chuck
Linda, 1975–76

Argentinean writer Jorge Luis Borges was all the rage in the 1960s and 1970s, and among his most famous works was the story *Pierre Menard, Author of the Quixote*. A modern writer, Menard set out to recreate Cervantes' masterpiece meticulously. Although every word was identical, the changing context made his a completely different work. Something of the same logic underlies the apparent perversity of the Superrealist project: what appears to be Realism is better seen as an elaborate game of allusion and irony.

Blown up to billboard-size, Chuck Close's portraits have all the impersonality of industrially produced advertising art, along with the intimacy of immediate connection. Many of his sitters are friends and fellow artists and their least blemishes are laboriously captured in loving detail. Like Roy Lichtenstein (1923–97), Close goes to enormous lengths to avoid any suggestion of painterly texture: he transfers a snapshot to a gigantic grid, then works with an airbrush to reproduce the sheer-smooth effects of the photographic original, and its flaws. Here, for example, the photograph's failure to cope with the stream of sunlight on the subject's hair, and the slight loss of focus about the shoulders, are both recreated by Close.

CREATED

New York

MEDIUM

Acrylic on canvas

PERIOD/SERIES/MOVEMENT

Superrealism

SIMILAR WORKS

Audrey Flack, *Lady Madonna*, c. 1972

Chuck Close *Born* 1940 Monroe, WA, USA

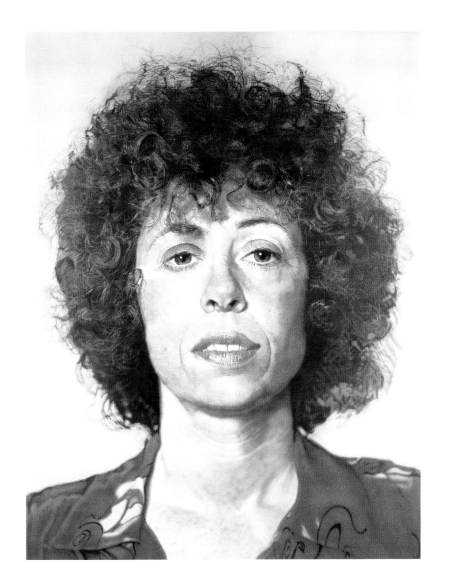

Hanson, Duane

Homeless Person, 1991

Superrealism in three dimensions, the style known as sculptural 'Verism' is the ultimate rejection of Abstraction, as one critic has pointed out. Yet the implied attack on modern art should not be misinterpreted: there is much more to this image than hard-hitting social commentary, although the plight of the homeless poor is undoubtedly one of the issues that it raises. There is humour here as well: the figure has found a 'home' of sorts in the art museum, whose wall wittily doubles as a surface for street graffiti. The same technique of 'life casting' is used by Hanson for the caricatured sculpture *American Tourists*, all swinging cameras and loud clothes, standing bemused in Edinburgh's National Gallery of Modern Art. John Ahearn's figures have provided the perfect way of taking art out into the community, in some of the most deprived inner-city neighbourhoods of America. Denver sculptor John de Andrea, meanwhile, has used the life-casting method to create nude figures in the classic tradition. It is quite wrong to see such works as 'anti-art': just like visual Superrealism, they are better regarded as elaborate puns on reality.

CREATED

New York

MEDIUM

Installation, mixed media

PERIOD/SERIES/MOVEMENT

Superrealism/Verist sculpture

SIMILAR WORKS

John Ahearn, *Veronica and her Mother*, 1988

Duane Hanson *Born* 1925 Minnesota, USA

Died 1996

Haring, Keith
Untitled, 1981

Even the most 'legitimate' artists have historically tended to live chaotic, 'Bohemian' lives, and since the Romantic era the raffish demimonde in which they have moved has to some extent been idealized in art and literature. The middle classes have, moreover, always had a way of envying the poor, if not their material privations, then at least their apparent freedom from respectable constraints. Hence the admiration felt by many artists for the untrammelled energy and undoubted ingenuity of the graffiti art that began to emblazon New York's subway trains in the 1970s. Intoxicated by the sense of freedom they found in such art, a number of American artists began to emulate it, both in public places and on canvases of their own. The most famous of these were Keith Haring (1958–90), an out-of-towner from Pennsylvania, and Jean-Michel Basquiat, an African-American artist of middle-class origins. British critics have dismissed Graffiti Art: at best it is bogus, they say; at worst a form of aesthetically sanctioned vandalism. Such criticism misses the main point: whether these intricate scribblings are authentic or not, works of great freshness and originality have been created.

CREATED

New York

MEDIUM

Oil and acrylic on canvas

PERIOD/SERIES/MOVEMENT

Graffiti Art

SIMILAR WORKS

Jean-Michel Basquiat, *Self-Portrait*, 1986

Keith Haring *Born* 1958 Kutztown, PA, USA

Died 1990

Sherman, Cindy
Untitled (Self-Portrait of Marilyn Monroe), 1982

Another artist, another Marilyn, but to a Postmodern sensibility such as Cindy Sherman's, the star is not just an image but a study in the ways of representation. It is also a look at the ways of representing women in particular. This image continues an extended series of 'movie stills' in which Sherman herself takes on the part of Hollywood actresses of the past. She has explored other stereotypical roles of womanhood as well, from the sultry pin-up to the medieval Madonna.

'Even though I've never thought of my work as feminist ...', says Sherman, 'everything in it was drawn from my observations as a woman in this culture.' Her works assume a certain critical distance from a mass iconography that Warhol, for example, was prepared simply to celebrate. Like many other women she has been concerned that images in the mass media have tended to objectify women, placing them in an essentially passive posture *vis à vis* the male 'gaze'. In commissions she has undertaken for the fashion industry, Sherman has sought to subvert conventions of this kind, blatantly caricaturing prevailing standards in feminine beauty.

CREATED

New York

MEDIUM

Ektachrome photograph

PERIOD/SERIES/MOVEMENT

Postmodernism

SIMILAR WORKS

Rineke Dijkstra, *Beach Portraits*, 1992–98

Jeff Wall, *A Sudden Gust of Wind (After Hokusai)*, 1993

Cindy Sherman *Born* 1954 Glen Ridge, NJ, USA

Basquiat, Jean-Michel
Arroz con Pollo, 1981

'My work has nothing to do with graffiti', Basquiat insisted. 'It is painting, and always has been.' The claim is characteristically confrontational, and so much at odds with the apparent record that it leads the reader to ponder just what the words 'graffiti' and 'painting' mean. This was, of course, the main purpose of Graffiti Art: it was the outsider's challenge to the cosily elitist world of conventional art. In Basquiat's work we see the influence not only of the street graffitists of his native city, but also of a primitivism that owes as much to Jean Dubuffet's (1901–85) Art Brut as it does to Africa.

Basquiat himself was half-Haitian and half-Puerto Rican, and saw himself as representing such marginalized groups. Angry and violent in its imagery, his work makes frequent reference to Haitian Voodoo traditions. Having attacked the art establishment, Basquiat was taken up by it, becoming, some complained, its pampered child. After four years he became a martyr to celebrity, dying of a heroin overdose. Nevertheless by then he had made an indelible, if controversial, mark on American art.

CREATED

New York

MEDIUM

Acrylic and paint stick on canvas

PERIOD/SERIES/MOVEMENT

Graffiti Art

SIMILAR WORKS

Keith Haring, *Subway Drawing*, 1980–81

Jean-Michel Basquiat *Born* 1960 Brooklyn, NY, USA

Died 1988

Gilbert and George

Helping Hands, 1982

Courtesy of Private Collection, Christie's Images Ltd/© Gilbert and George

'Gilbert and George': the suggestion of the comedy duo is certainly deliberate on the part of what has been the great double-act on the British artistic stage since they came together at St Martin's School of Art in London in 1967. The association is appropriate, given that they made their name in Performance Art, an activity that involves staging events (or 'stunts', critics sneer) that it is hoped will provide, at least momentarily, a new and different perspective on reality. The organization of such events is at least as old as Dada, but dedicated Performance Art was very much a product of the video age.

The comics' billing is also apposite because humour is central to what Gilbert and George do: poking fun at the pretensions of an art establishment they feel takes itself far too seriously, and seeking to find an art that will genuinely delight and entertain.

During the 1980s they turned increasingly to two-dimensional works, and often, like this one, they incorporated paint and photomontage. This too is a performance, however, with the staidly-suited artists themselves as its subject, comically hindered by all those 'helping hands'.

CREATED

London

MEDIUM

Photomontage

PERIOD/SERIES/MOVEMENT

Body Art/Performance Art/Art For All

SIMILAR WORKS

Bruce Nauman, *From Hand to Mouth*, 1967

Mark Wallinger, *Angel*, 1997

Gilbert Proesch *Born* 1942 Dolomite, Italy   **George Pasmore** *Born* 1943 Barnstaple, England

Saville, Jenny
Untitled, 1990

Courtesy of Private Collection, Lefevre Fine Art Ltd., London/www.bridgeman.co.uk/© Jenny Saville

The Marxist writer and critic John Berger caused a considerable stir in 1972 when he presented a landmark TV series on art with accompanying essays called *Ways of Seeing*. He made many contentious claims in what amounted to a sustained prosecution of art – both 'high' and 'low' – for collaborating with the enemy, wealth and property. However, his most far-reaching criticisms were reserved for the institution of the female nude. Even in its most supposedly exalted instances, he suggested, it amounted to 'soft porn' and implied that female beauty was about passivity and availability.

He made his case crudely, perhaps, and yet in the decades since he has found broad acceptance: part of the problem, of course, was that artistic conventions were for centuries set exclusively by men. A key challenge for those women artists, who have made their way on to the scene in more recent times, has accordingly been to find a more acceptable way of presenting the female body. Many have found other subjects, of course, yet that is arguably to efface or even erase it: Jenny Saville has tackled the problem head-on in her emotionally charged 'Neo-Expressionist' self-portraits.

CREATED

London

MEDIUM

Oil on canvas

PERIOD/SERIES/MOVEMENT

Neo-Expressionism

SIMILAR WORKS

Eric Fischl, *The Travel of Romance*, 1994

Jenny Saville *Born* 1970 Cambridge, England

Auerbach, Frank

Head of J. Y. M. I, 1981

Nothing could be more Postmodern than the past, supposedly so fixed and immutable, but actually altered by every new development, every shift in perception, every insight. The truth of this is illustrated by the way in which the turn towards 'Neo-Expressionism' in the 1980s prompted a rediscovery and revaluation of the Expressionism of yore. Certainly that was so in England, where the works of old stagers of the London School underwent a comprehensive reassessment, Frank Auerbach in particular. It was not so much that his paintings had changed – this 1981 work might easily have been produced several decades earlier. Nevertheless the scene had changed around it, and context, culturally, is all.

The sweeping brushstrokes and densely textured surface are here the same as ever, yet this portrait comes across as reinvigorated, newly challenging work. 'Narrative without storytelling' was the essence of Neo-Expressionist art, said British sculptor Anish Kapoor (b. 1954): 'that which allows one to bring in psychology, fear, death and love in as direct a way as possible.' It is no surprise that a generation grown weary of pallid 'purity' in art should have been drawn to the raw emotions of Expressionism.

CREATED

London

MEDIUM

Oil on canvas

PERIOD/SERIES/MOVEMENT

Neo-Expressionism

SIMILAR WORKS

Lucian Freud, *Naked Man, Back View*, 1991–92

Frank Auerbach *Born* 1931 Berlin, Germany

Hodgkin, Howard

Robyn Denny and Katherine Reid, 1973–75

Howard Hodgkin was another beneficiary of the rediscovery of Expressionist values in the 1980s, his response at the time being to create bigger, bolder works. Yet Neo-Expressionist revisionism also brought a re-presentation of earlier works, such as this one, and a re-appreciation of Hodgkin's powerful use of colour.

Like so much of Hodgkin's work, this painting is both abstract and figurative in its intention, and he himself insisted that his was representational art. In the true Expressionist spirit, however, he set out to capture not the scene before him but the 'emotional situation'. Hence the paradox of a portrait, the subjects of which are indistinguishably subsumed into a wider pattern. As with all Expressionist portraiture we are left to wonder whether the emotions are those of subjects or artist (or some sort of aggregate), yet that only lends an additional and intriguing dimension to the work. Just as intriguing are the tantalizing hints of figuration we are proffered here: is that the seated form of somebody in red trousers, just left of centre? There are elements both of human forms and their domestic setting: brick-like stripes on the right and the suggestion of a staircase on the left, for example.

CREATED

London

MEDIUM

Oil on wood

PERIOD/SERIES/MOVEMENT

Neo-Expressionism

SIMILAR WORKS

Patrick Heron, *The Shapes of Colour*, 1978

Howard Hodgkin *Born* 1932 London, England

Hume, Gary
Water Painting, 1999

Courtesy of Tate, London 2005/© Gary Hume

The capacity of modern industrial technologies to mass-produce individual images on an infinite scale fascinated the first Pop Artists. Warhol's rows of repeated celebrities, from Elvis to Jackie Kennedy and from Marilyn to Mao, were the results of precisely this preoccupation. Yet, as the work of Cindy Sherman and Jenny Saville shows, a new generation of artists was less content simply to celebrate mass culture. Increasingly art was asking questions about the influence these images had on individual lives, both those of the stars, celebrities and models it represented and of the wider public who were its consumers.

First traced from magazines and newspapers on to film and then projected on to aluminium panels and reproduced in high-gloss household paint, Gary Hume's works have all the sheen and glamour of their originals. Rather than repeating identical images sequentially, in regimented rows, however, Hume overlaps multiple figures palimpsestically to produce a confusion of undifferentiated bodily bits and pieces. The effect, at first glance alluring, is on closer consideration disturbing: where are the individual subjects in this glamorous chaos?

CREATED

London

MEDIUM

Household paint on aluminium panel

PERIOD/SERIES/MOVEMENT

Britart/Young British Artists

SIMILAR WORKS

Andy Warhol, *Double Jackie*, 1965

Gary Hume *Born* Kent, England, 1962

Modern Art

Abstract,
Colour & Form

Balla, Giacomo

The Speed of an Automobile, 1913

At their most facile, the Futurists were interested chiefly in big bangs, powerful engines and the sheer destructive force of new technologies. Yet the school had more thoughtful adherents, artists of real imaginition and originality, and they were interested in opening up a genuinely new dimension in art. They felt strongly that it needed to move on from its traditional concern with outline shape and solid mass, or even the light effects that had interested the Impressionists. Instead they considered that artists should engage directly with dynamism and energy.

Painters such as Giacomo Balla carried figurative art to the borders of abstraction – and, increasingly, beyond – in their attempts to capture what they saw as the universal 'vitalizing' principle. It was a time when moving pictures were being made for the first time, and film frames were being used to elucidate the mysteries of movement in animals: this was an area where scientific and artistic interest coincided. Balla followed such researches closely, but he never forgot that he was a painter, first and foremost: along with energy there is also wit and even lyricism in his work.

CREATED

Rome

MEDIUM

Oil on card

PERIOD/SERIES/MOVEMENT

Futurism

SIMILAR WORKS

Umberto Boccioni, *Materia*, 1912 (

Giacomo Balla *Born* 1871 Turin, Italy

Died 1958

Russolo, Luigi
Music, 1911

Like Giacomo (1871–1958) and the other Futurists, Luigi Russolo took representational art to the very borders of abstraction, but he took pictorial art to another frontier too. Music, his theme in this spectacular (and, by Futurist standards, exceptionally colourful) work, was the first love and lifelong obsession of this painter. The counterpointing of regularity and freedom that we see suggested in this picture was plainly one of its attractions, as perhaps was the way it could combine complete impersonality with intimacy and warmth. Not surprisingly Russolo was a composer as well as an artist and 'Futurist Music' began, and unfortunately ended, with his work, very little of which survives. Easy as it is to deride what was certainly one of the twentieth century's great creative cul-de-sacs, it is worth recording that such masters as Maurice Ravel and Igor Stravinsky attended performances of his compositions and were much taken with what they heard. In addition, the advent of electronic music has brought a renewed interest in his work. We may not have heard the last of Russolo the composer, and in the meantime the painter has left us several remarkable works.

CREATED

Milan

MEDIUM

Oil on canvas

PERIOD/SERIES/MOVEMENT

Futurism

SIMILAR WORKS

Carlo Carrà, *Pursuit*, 1915

Luigi Russolo *Born* 1885 Portogravo, Italy

Died 1947

Kandinsky, Wassily
Composition No. 7, 1913

'An empty canvas, apparently really empty, that says nothing and is without significance. Almost dull, in fact. In reality, however, crammed with thousands of undertone tensions and full of expectancy. Slightly apprehensive lest it should be outraged. Yet docile enough. Ready to do what is required of it, and only asking for consideration ... An empty canvas is a living wonder.' Thus wrote the great Expressionist Wassily Kandinsky, towards the end of his extraordinary career in 1937. For him wonder was the great theme of art: art was a spiritual, mystical experience, both in creation and contemplation. He and his fellow founders of Der Blaue Reiter shared comparatively little in terms of technique, but were united by a sense that the artist should have free rein to find whatever form suited his or her need for self-expression. In his case that would eventually mean abstraction, rich and colourful, although in the movement's early years he still offered tantalizing, semi-figurative forms. The sense of wonder was the same, however, as more crowded canvases were surely never seen; every space seemingly a painting waiting to happen.

CREATED

Munich

MEDIUM

Oil on canvas

PERIOD/SERIES/MOVEMENT

Der Blaue Reiter/Expressionism

SIMILAR WORKS

Franz Marc, *The Unfortunate Land of Tyrol*, 1913

Wassily Kandinsky *Born* 1866 Moscow, Russia

Died 1944

Kupka, Frantisek
Study on Amorpha, c. 1912

Frantisek Kupka's marvellous works have made him one of the best-known members of the school of Orphism (see page 92), a group that sought to find the most musical and spiritual elements of the soul through art. His own artistic quest, however, was focused more narrowly on that mysterious concept or spirit to which he gave the name 'Amorpha'. This seems, as its name implies, to have encompassed not only those qualities customarily associated with Orphism, but also those suggested by the Greek element 'morph', or 'change'. His works are beautiful studies in amorphousness, in the transition from one shape into another, and in the interlocking and interpenetration of these different forms.

As with Orphism in general, the riddling incomprehensibility of the theory is not reflected in the stunning simplicity of the work itself. Kupka's paintings are masterpieces, beautifully economic and perfectly poised. He saw himself as a 'colour symphonist', which was not in fact an altogether unjustified claim on the part of one of the most underrated figures in twentieth-century art.

CREATED

Paris

MEDIUM

Gouache, watercolour and pencil on paper

PERIOD/SERIES/MOVEMENT

Orphism

SIMILAR WORKS

Robert Delaunay, *Simultaneous Contrasts: Sun and Moon*, 1913

Frantisek Kupka *Born* 1871 Opocno, Bohemia

Died 1957

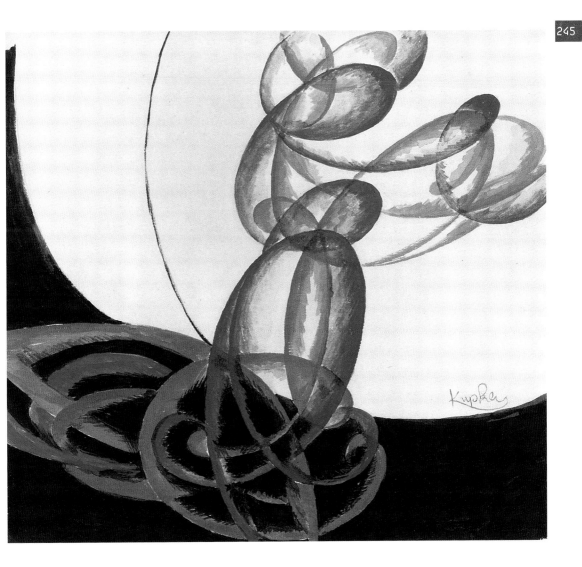

Delaunay, Sonia

Ses Peintures, Ses Objets, Ses Tissus Simultanes, Ses Modes: Twenty Color Plates c. 1912–25

The allocation of artists to 'schools' or 'movements' is often an arbitrary convenience as most are individualists by nature. Moreover, their work changes and develops as they themselves grow older and as influences come crowding in upon their lives, so an energetic artist may belong to several schools or none in the course of a career. Sonia Delaunay is a good example: she has gone down in art history as an Orphist, a justifiable categorization as far as it goes. She was the wife of Robert Delaunay (1885–1941), the movement's leader, and his influence is evident here. Yet if she had married the man, she certainly had not married his movement. Earlier in the century, Sonia had been strongly influenced by the Fauves, an influence she was obviously slow to put aside. Orphism was generally less precisely defined than is often assumed, hence the peripheral involvement of avowed Cubists such as Francis Picabia (1879–1953). An artist like Sonia Delaunay would ultimately always remain her own woman with her own ideas.

CREATED

Paris

MEDIUM

Pochoir

PERIOD/SERIES/MOVEMENT

Orphism

Sonia Delaunay *Born* 1885 Ukraine, Russia

Died 1979

1915

Larionov, Mikhail

Rayonist Composition, c. 1913

At first lovers and life partners before marrying many decades later, Mikhail Larionov and Natalia Goncharova (1881–1962) more or less launched the modern movement in Russian art. Russian intellectuals since Alexander Herzen (1812–70) had deplored their countrymen's cultural 'cringe' in the face of Western fashions, so it is hardly surprising that the two should have started out by looking to their own country's folk traditions as inspiration for their 'Jack of Diamonds' school.

Had Russian inferiority lain only in the area of art, this might have been an adequate response. But with the country stalled in economic and technological backwardness, as well as being in the increasingly chaotic lead up to a revolution, the appeal of modernity – a Western monopoly – proved irresistible. Hence the introduction of Rayonism, named for its concern with the behaviour of rays of light, but really a Russian version of Italian Futurism. Rayonist rhetoric echoed that of F. T. Marinetti (1876–1944), albeit with some Russian sartorial stipulations all its own: 'We declare the genius of our days to be: trousers, jackets, shows, tramways, buses, aeroplanes, railways, magnificent ships – what an enchantment!'

CREATED

Moscow

MEDIUM

Watercolour on paper

PERIOD/SERIES/MOVEMENT

Rayonism

SIMILAR WORKS

Natalia Goncharova, *Rayonism: Blue-Green Forest*, 1913; dated 1911

Mikhail Larionov *Born* 1881 near Odessa, Russia

Died 1964

Malevich, Kasimir

Suprematist Composition, 1915

Another 'Jack of Diamonds' veteran, along with Larionov and Goncharova, Malevich parted company with his former companions in the years that followed. By 1915 he had founded his own artistic school, to which he gave the title 'Suprematism'. Confining itself to geometric forms, juxtaposing planes of pure colour, Suprematism anticipates *De Stijl* in certain ways. As with the later movement, while the regularity of the shapes involved may appear to suggest a rationalistic approach to art, it actually comes close to mysticism in its rhetoric. 'Under Suprematism', said Malevich, 'I understand the supremacy of pure feeling in creative art.' Plane shapes provided the best vehicle for that feeling because they had none of those irregularities or particular details that for Malevich, as for Piet Mondrian (1872–1944), gave a distracting impression that something was being depicted. A pure black square was, he insisted, the true 'zero of form', the white space that stretched away behind it the empty void. 'Only when the habit of one's consciousness to see in paintings bits of nature, madonnas and shameless nudes has disappeared, shall we see a pure-painting composition', he maintained.

CREATED

Moscow

MEDIUM

Oil on canvas

PERIOD/SERIES/MOVEMENT

Suprematism

SIMILAR WORKS

László Moholy-Nagy, *K VII*, 1922

Kasimir Malevich *Born* 1878 Kiev, Russia

Died 1935

Lissitzky, El
Proun 12 E, 1923

El Lissitzky made a series of these 'Prouns' – his own little genre of playful, puzzling games of line and plane and geometric form – whose name was supposedly an acronym for 'Projects For the Affirmation of the New' in Russian. They constituted, he said, a meeting-point between art and architecture. That such a meeting was desirable went without saying in the political context of the time: art was idle, but architecture was constructive. In the years following the Revolution, building was the predominant activity in the Soviet Union, in both the most literal and the most metaphorical of senses. Apartment blocks were being built to rehouse the people, the economic infrastructure was being modernized, a new society was actively under construction. As proclaimed by Vladimir Tatlin, Constructivism gave the artist a real part to play in this great venture – his or her contribution could be made on an equal footing with other workers. Lissitzky's Prouns were directly inspired by this excitement, this will to build, but they transcend the immediate context that produced them. Long after the edifice of Soviet Communism came crashing down, they appear as fresh as ever, thanks to their classic poise, ingenuity and wit.

CREATED

Moscow

MEDIUM

Oil on canvas

PERIOD/SERIES/MOVEMENT

Constructivism

SIMILAR WORKS

Varvara Stepanova, *Figure*, 1921

Eliezer (El) Lissitzky *Born near Smolensk, Russia*

Died 1941

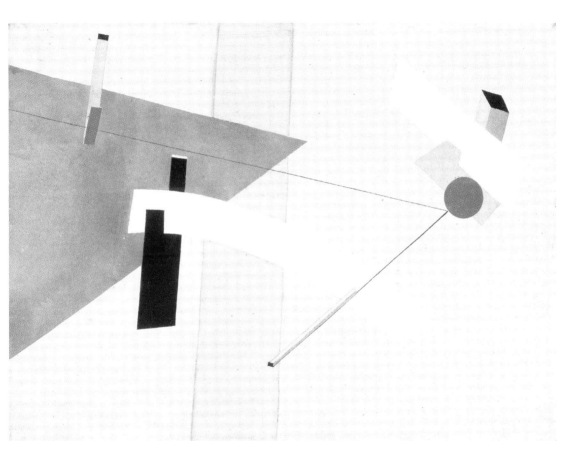

Atkinson, Lawrence

Abstract, c. 1915–20

Lawrence Atkinson had regarded himself as an 'English Cubist' for some years before throwing in his lot with Percy Wyndham Lewis's (1884–1957) Vorticist movement. Traces of the Cubist style still linger here, not just in the simple squareness of the forms but also in the space allowed to surround the central form in what, by Vorticist standards, is a comparatively quiet and uncrowded canvas. Along with the French school's preoccupation with the presentation of three-dimensional forms in space, however, a concern can clearly be seen to capture tension, energy and dynamism.

Like the Futurists, by whom they were very obviously much influenced, the Vorticists took a savage delight in power, strength and speed. Characteristically Wyndham Lewis called upon his followers to emulate 'the forms of machinery, factories, new and vaster buildings, bridges and works'. He implied not only a new subject for art, but also a new type of practitioner: no longer an effete aesthete but a tough-minded engineer in plane, line and colour. Although ultimately an abstract, this work by Atkinson is clearly representational enough to suggest some sort of construction along these lines.

CREATED

London

MEDIUM

Oil on panel

PERIOD/SERIES/MOVEMENT

Vorticism

SIMILAR WORKS

David Bomberg, *The Mud Bath*, 1914

Lawrence Atkinson *Born* 1873 Manchester, England

Died 1931

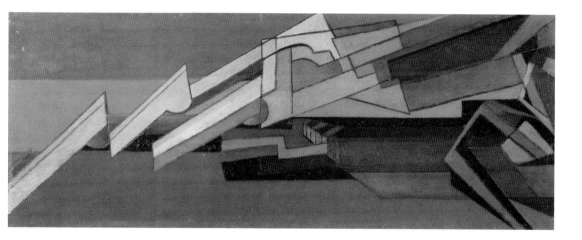

Huszár, Vilmos

Composition, c. 1955–60

Hungarian-born Vilmos Huszár came to the Netherlands in 1906, and his first profession was that of architecture. He would never be a full-time painter, but then the *De Stijl* movement that he was to help to found in 1917 had ambitions extending far beyond the walls of the art gallery. Huszár, Mondrian and their followers set out not just to create images but to reform lives, bringing a new balance both to the existence of the individual and to that of society as a whole. In keeping with that vision, Huszár in particular worked across a wide range of different fields, embracing everything from painting to garden design. *De Stijl* was as much an architectural school as it was an 'art' movement, with such distinguished adherents as J. J. P. Oud, Robert Van't Hoff, Jan Wils and Gerrit Rietveld attempting to put its principles into practice. The movement had its own poet, Antony Kok, and even a philosopher – or theologian – M. H. J. Schoenmakers. *De Stijl* was not just a 'style' in the usual artistic sense, but in intention at least it was a complete approach to life, with implications for every man and woman and society as a whole.

CREATED

Amsterdam

MEDIUM

Oil on panel

PERIOD/SERIES/MOVEMENT

De Stijl

SIMILAR WORKS

Georges Vantongerloo, *Composition II, Indigo Violet Derived from Equilateral Triangle*, 1921

Vilmos Huszár *Born* 1884 Budapest, Hungary

Died 1960

van Doesburg, Theo

Contra-Composition of Dissonances, XVI, 1925

'The object of nature is man,' wrote Theo van Doesburg in 1919. 'The object of man is style.' The aphorism sums up De Stijl succinctly, but needs unpacking. Style, van Doesburg suggested, as 'positively expressed in modern plasticity', was a 'well-balanced proportion between peculiarity and generalness'. Too great a concern with the surface, as exemplified in representational art, distracted attention from the inner spirituality of things. Art, he felt, should not be about objectivity but transcendence; beauty lay not in verisimilitude but balance. *De Stijl*, as we have seen, saw the universe as being organized in geometric forms, from which essentials the irregularities of observed reality were only a distraction. The task before the artist was to offer glimpses of that underlying equilibrium in pictures that would inspire viewers to strive to bring about a similar balance in their lives, their society and their built environment. This was an evangelizing art, then, which conducted itself very much as a religion, even to the extent of having schisms – Mondrian left the movement in 1925, apparently affronted at van Doesburg's unorthodox use of diagonals.

CREATED

Amsterdam

MEDIUM

Oil on canvas

PERIOD/SERIES/MOVEMENT

De Stijl

SIMILAR WORKS

Piet Mondrian, *Composition in Colour A*, 1917

Theo van Doesburg (born Christiaan Küppers) *Born* 1883 Utrecht, Netherlands

Died 1931

Moholy-Nagy, László
Architektur I, 1922

'Hungarian Activism' was briefly the particular form in which the Modernist wave hit Hungary, a response to Cubism, Expressionism, Futurism and all the other new schools. As in Russia, the embrace of the new in art went along with specifically socialist political ideals. The movement was led by Lajos Kassák, who published a famous journal, *MA* ('Today'). Its intention according to a contributor was, 'not ... to establish a new school of art but a completely new conception of art and the world'.

In 1919 it looked as though he might just get his way: a Soviet Republic was proclaimed in Hungary, but it collapsed completely within four months of its creation and many artists were compelled to go into exile. Perhaps the movement's most important talent, Moholy-Nagy was among them. At first he set up in Vienna, then in 1921 he went to Berlin, but he was moving on both geographically and artistically all the time. Within a year of creating this work he would be in Weimar, a master at the Bauhaus, where he would at least help bring about 'a new conception of art'.

CREATED

Berlin

MEDIUM

Oil and silver paint on canvas

PERIOD/SERIES/MOVEMENT

Hungarian Activism/Constructivism/Bauhaus

SIMILAR WORKS

Lajos Kassák, *Pictorial Architecture*, 1922

János Máttis-Teutsch, *Untitled*, 1925

László Moholy-Nagy *Born* 1895 Bácsborsod, Hungary

Died 1946

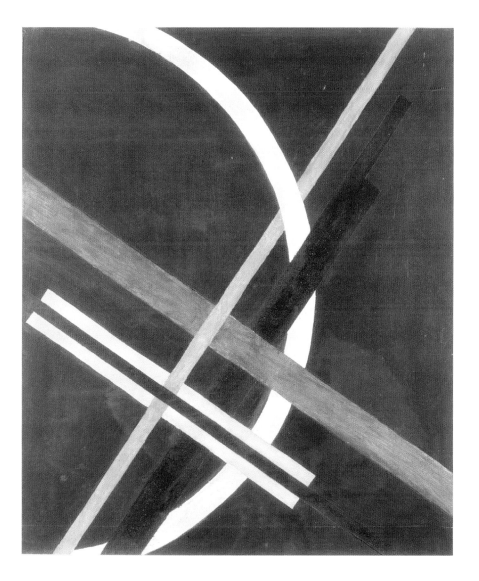

Gorky, Arshile
Untitled, 1946

Arshile Gorky's sickness and ultimately his suicide deprived twentieth-century art of a great talent, even before it could ever really be fulfilled. Although Gorky was a man with more than his share of demons (his mother had been murdered in the Turkish attacks on the Armenians, the century's first great atrocity, and, just a boy, he had made his way to America with his younger sister), he was an ebullient figure. He was also an inspiring polemicist for the artistic revolutions of his age. 'The twentieth century!' he enthused, 'What intensity, what activity, what restless, nervous energy!' He might, of course, have been summing up his own work.

What heights he might one day have reached is speculative; his place in art history is assured as a founder (some say *the* founder) of Abstract Impressionism. He got there via Cubism ('Has there in six centuries been better art...?') and was influenced along the way by his friend Stuart Davis's theories that the juxtaposition of colours could signify space. Yet his work is as remarkable for the influence it exerted on others, most importantly perhaps on Willem de Kooning (1904–97).

CREATED

New York

MEDIUM

Oil on canvas

PERIOD/SERIES/MOVEMENT

Abstract Expressionism

SIMILAR WORKS

Stuart Davis, *Report from Rockport*, 1940

Arshile Gorky (born Vosdanig Manoog Adoian) *Born* 1904 Armenia

Died 1948

Nicholson, Ben

Painted Relief – Plover's Egg Blue, 1940

The product of an artistic family – both his father and mother had been painters – Ben Nicholson had the best imaginable upbringing for a painter. Nevertheless, nothing could have prepared him for the experience that awaited him when he went to visit Mondrian's studio in Paris in 1934. The white space in which the master worked astounded him almost as much as the pictures did. Afterwards he sat at a pavement café in a trance, with 'an astonishing feeling of quiet and repose'.

This is the rhetoric of religious conversion and in a sense that is what it was, although it was what he had seen that had moved him, not the mystic thinking it was intended to embody. Nicholson did feel an almost missionary sense of the importance of art, though: 'A Raphael is not a painting in the National Gallery,' he said, 'it is an active force in our lives.' His vision was broad and tolerant: despite aspiring in his own work to the austere rigour of Concrete Art (see page 48), he encouraged younger artists of all kinds.

CREATED

St Ives, Cornwall

MEDIUM

Oil on carved panel

PERIOD/SERIES/MOVEMENT

Concrete Art/St Ives School

SIMILAR WORKS

Max Bill, *Rhythm in Four Squares*, 1943

Ben Nicholson *Born* 1894 Denham, England

Died 1982

Wols

Composition, 1947

Courtesy of Hamburg Kunsthalle, Hamburg, Germany/www.bridgeman.co.uk/© ADAGP, Paris and DACS, London 2005

'Wols' had been pursuing his studies in art for almost two decades before he came to prominence in his final years. He had briefly studied at the Bauhaus in the 1930s, but left Germany disenchanted at the rise of Hitler. Travelling first to Paris, he had moved from there to Barcelona, only to find himself imprisoned for his political activities. The outbreak of civil war in Spain saw him unceremoniously deported to France, but before long the Second World War had begun and he was then interned. Freed in 1940, he stayed in the south of France, keeping his head down. Not until the late 1940s was he able to launch anything like a career, and even then he was hampered by his diffidence and by his impatience with the business of being an artist: only after his death did his works receive wide attention.

Given his self-effacement in life and the way he had, as it were, sidled up to art over so many years, the explosive boldness of Wols' works is quite astounding. Although wildly unplanned they still contrive to suggest organic forms, and their intensity makes them linger in the mind.

CREATED

Paris

MEDIUM

Oil on canvas

PERIOD/SERIES/MOVEMENT

Art Informel

SIMILAR WORKS

Hans Hartung, *T-1954-20*, 1954

Wols (born Alfred Otto Wolfgang Schultze) *Born* 1913 Berlin, Germany

Died 1951

Heron, Patrick

Cobalt with Blue and Yellow, 1968

Patrick Heron is loosely associated with the St Ives School, founded by Ben Nicholson and Barbara Hepworth (1903–75) in the 1940s – not that it is possible to be anything but loosely associated with so tolerant and wide-ranging a group of artists. Only a common interest in abstraction really connects the works of the different members, and Heron has produced some of the most striking abstract works of the postwar period.

His chief interest is in colour. He had early interests in Georges Braque (1882–1963) and in the Fauves, and this has always been given primacy in his paintings. Hence a work such as this, which can be seen as a painting in Tachist style, starting out from – and in some sense dictated by – the initial stain or blot (French *tâche*) made by the paint on the canvas. Heron's impact on art in both Britain and North America has been considerable, not just as practising painter but also as critic. In such roles he has helped on the one hand to bring British artists up to speed with developments in the United States, and on the other to 'fly the flag' for British painting.

CREATED

Zennor, Cornwall

MEDIUM

Oil on canvas

PERIOD/SERIES/MOVEMENT

Art Informel/St Ives School

SIMILAR WORKS

Pierre Soulages, *Painting*, 1956

Patrick Heron *Born* 1920 Leeds, England

Died 1999

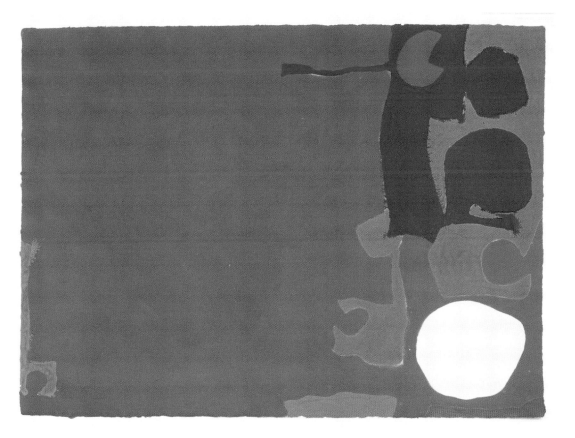

Rothko, Mark
Untitled, 1951

To confront a Mark Rothko work such as this one is to feel caught up in a real confrontation. Critic David Sylvester has remarked on the 'emphatic frontality' of the artist's work. 'We are', he writes, 'faced with a highly ambiguous presence which seems, on the one hand, ethereal, empty, on the other solid and imposing, like a megalith.' It possesses, Sylvester concludes, the sort of sublimity to be found in a wild landscape and clearly springs from the Romantic tradition in western art.

More technically, works in this style are known as 'Colour Field Painting' because the work is seen as a single, continuous field without obvious focus or compositional hierarchy. The term derives from 'Field Painting', which attempted to achieve a comparable effect with abstract forms. Helen Frankenthaler's 'stain painting' (see page 138) was to take this style another step further in the 1960s. Yet Sylvester is surely right: Rothko is a Romantic and the essence of his work escapes such analysis. No real work of art can satisfactorily be summed up in technical terms, perhaps, but the attempt in Rothko's case falls especially short.

CREATED

New York

MEDIUM

Acrylic on canvas

PERIOD/SERIES/MOVEMENT

Abstract Expressionism/Colour Field Painting

SIMILAR WORKS

Hans Hofmann, *The Gate*, 1959–60

Adolph Gottlieb, *Three Discs*, 1960

Mark Rothko (born Marcus Rothkowitz) *Born* 1903 Dvinsk, Russia

Died 1970

Newman, Barnett

Be I (Second Version), 1970

'Aesthetics is to the artist as ornithology is for the birds': Barnett Newman's put-down for critics and philosophers of art is justly famed. Despite his proclamation, few practising painters have, in truth, worried away at theoretical problems as assiduously as he has: his is by any standards a highly intellectualized approach to art. 'The basis of an aesthetic act is the pure idea', he writes. 'But the pure idea is, of necessity, an aesthetic act.' This is the contradiction against which Newman's imagination runs up repeatedly, and with which he wrestles daily in his work. 'It is only the pure idea that has meaning', he maintains. 'Everything else has everything else.'

Such a determined insistence on the abstract idea to the exclusion of all objective reference, all particularizing detail, is reminiscent of the rhetoric of Mondrian and Theo van Doesburg. His works echo theirs as well, although they are if anything even simpler, as we see here. Newman is heir to their mystical leanings, but in his case this is articulated in an interest in the largely discarded notion of the 'sublime', as something greater and grander than humankind.

CREATED

New York

MEDIUM

Acrylic on canvas

PERIOD/SERIES/MOVEMENT

Abstract Expressionism/Colour Field Painting

SIMILAR WORKS

Mark Rothko, *Black on Maroon (Two Openings in Black Over Wine)*, 1958

Barnett Newman *Born* 1905 New York, USA

Died 1970

Motherwell, Robert

Elegy, 1948

An 'elegy', traditionally, is a song or poem for the dead, and a sense of loss all but pervades Robert Motherwell's work. Indeed he is best known for a lengthy series of 'Elegies for the Spanish Republic' – stark, simple paintings, largely in black and white. Motherwell mourned those who fell fighting for democracy in the Spanish Civil War (1936–39), but his series is dedicated not to them, but to the ideal for which they fought. Bereavement can be intellectual, political, cultural, in other words – the fact that it is not personal does not necessarily make it less emotional. The artist has always felt philosophically isolated, 'unwedded to the universe', as Motherwell puts it, his work an attempt to bind himself into the wider scheme of things.

The need for a sense of 'belonging' was clearly important to Motherwell. His work, although always abstract, tended to make reference to historical events or works of literature. Some contemporaries felt he took himself too seriously, was too conscious of his place in the artistic tradition, but this was just another mark of his sense of intellectual isolation and his longing for cultural 'company'.

CREATED

New York

MEDIUM

Paper collage and gouache on masonite

PERIOD/SERIES/MOVEMENT

Abstract Expressionism

SIMILAR WORKS

William Baziotes, *Watercolor #4*, 1958

Robert Motherwell *Born* 1915 Aberdeen, WA, USA

Died 1991

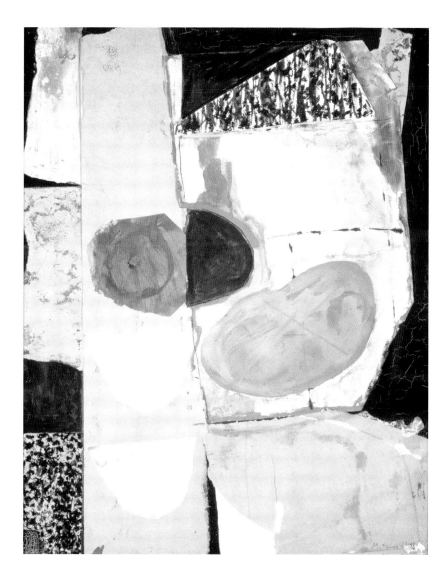

Still, Clyfford
1955-D, 1955

'And the artist today, who is he? A lower-middle class Christ who can sub in a pinch as a baubled court jester? An intuitive boob? ... A mystic slob, perhaps vomiting on a bed for the benefit of a dinner party? Or is he a spaniel for old ladies?'. Clyfford Still burst on to the American art scene with all the force of an Old Testament prophet and, as is the way with prophets, what he had to say was not always welcome. He adapted to his role with gusto, thunderously denouncing the work of contemporaries whom in mellower moments he counted among his friends, and attaching all sorts of conditions as to how and where his works could be displayed. In 1961 he ostentatiously withdrew from the New York art scene, setting up in Maryland where he could pursue his work in peace. In retrospect he can be seen as belonging to that mini-tradition of modern painters in whose semi-religious work, plainness and purity of colour is next to godliness; a tradition taking in Mondrian, of course, as well as Abstract Expressionists such as Mark Rothko and Barnett Newman.

CREATED

New York

MEDIUM

Acrylic on canvas

PERIOD/SERIES/MOVEMENT

Abstract Expressionism/Colour Field Painting

SIMILAR WORKS

Barnett Newman, *Vir Heroicus Sublimis* ('Sublime, Heroic Man'), 1950–51

Clyfford Still *Born* 1904 Grandin, ND, USA

Died 1980

Pollock, Jackson
Number 6, 1948

'New arts need new techniques', Jackson Pollock told an interviewer in 1950. 'The modern artist cannot express this age, the airplane, the atom bomb, the radio, in the old forms of the Renaissance or of any other past culture.' How far any of these things were expressed in the splashes and squiggles of 'Jack the Dripper' has of course been hotly debated ever since. His real object was not to depict his age but to express its preoccupations and its energy. The means he found to do this became known as 'Action Painting' because, rather as *Art Informel* had done, it placed its emphasis on the actions and gestures by which the paint was applied and the picture made. Laying out his working surfaces flat on the floor – that way he felt he could approach them from any and every direction without privileging a particular orientation – Pollock dribbled wet paint with a stick or directly from the can. He is guilty as charged of creating nonsense, in that his paintings offer no articulate meaning, but they are fraught with energy, tension, passion and drama.

CREATED

New York

MEDIUM

Oil on paper laid down on canvas

PERIOD/SERIES/MOVEMENT

Abstract Expressionism

SIMILAR WORKS

Willem de Kooning, *Composition*, 1955

Jackson Pollock *Born* 1912 Cody, WY, USA

Died 1956

Klein, Yves
Ant 50, 1960

Yves Klein was an artistic entrepreneur, even patenting his own paint ('International Klein Blue') and it can hardly be denied that he was also something of a showman. *Ant 50* is one of a series of monochrome works created with what he called 'living brushes', in this case the naked body of model Héléna. She was daubed with paint then placed upon the paper, while a musical piece of Klein's composition (the 'Monotone Symphony': a single sustained note, alternating with lengthy silences) played in the background. The resulting picture shows her straddled legs below, her breasts at centre and her hands at either side above, along with a barely perceptible lipstick mark.

A gimmick? Perhaps, yet such *anthropométries* were a logical product of what Klein's friend the critic Pierre Restany had christened the *Nouveau Réalisme*. Rejecting a tendency towards abstraction, which Restany, Klein and their circle saw as divorcing art from life, they sought new ways of coming at reality. Despite all his charlatanism, Klein's search for an art that would be free from subjectivity aligns him with many of the more obviously 'serious' artists of the century.

CREATED

Paris

MEDIUM

Blue pigment, synthetic resin – and a trace of lipstick – on paper laid down on canvas

PERIOD/SERIES/MOVEMENT

Nouveau Réalisme ('New Realism')

SIMILAR WORKS

Arman, *Doorbells*, 1961

Yves Klein *Born* 1928 Nice, France

Died 1962

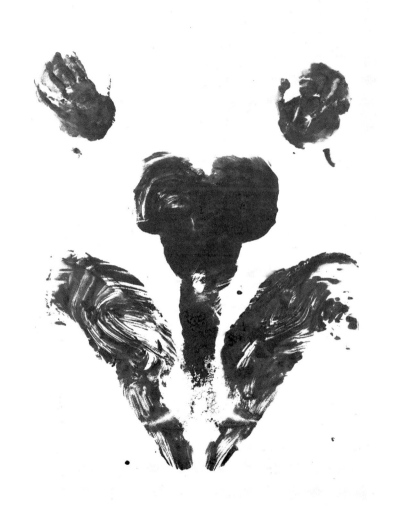

Dine, Jim

Flo-Marker Hearts, 1969

The subject matter is very recognizably that of Pop Art, but the effect is altogether more painterly than is to be found in the famous works of Andy Warhol (1928–87) or Roy Lichtenstein (1923–98). It recalls, indeed, the intense canvases of the Abstract Expressionists. A major figure on the Pop Art scene of the 1960s, Dine was a pioneer of the 'Happening', a staged event involving bystanders in a sort of organized spontaneity and the inspiration for later Performance Art.

The nature of such creations is that they are one-offs, their unpredictability and impermanence representing a conscious rejection of old-fashioned artistic conventions by which the artist aspired to complete control and a 'classic' beauty that would transcend time. Jim Dine turns a Janus face to art, embracing the new aesthetic in all its unruliness and its delight in the ephemeral, without relinquishing his concern to create beauty of a more traditional sort. In this he resembles R. B. Kitaj (1927–94), an acknowledged influence, with whom Dine came into contact when both were working in England in the 1960s.

CREATED

London

MEDIUM

Watercolour on paper

PERIOD/SERIES/MOVEMENT

Pop Art

SIMILAR WORKS

Ed Ruscha, *Ace*, 1962–63

Jim Dine *Born* 1935 Cincinnati, OH, USA

Vasarely, Victor
Vega Pal, 1969

'Op Art' was so-called by the media partly because it concerned itself with optical effects, but also by derivation from Pop Art, after which it was 'the next best thing'. The name makes perfect sense on the first account, but the second association is less fortunate since there was little originally connecting the two styles.

Victor Vasarely, the generally acknowledged founder of the movement, had worked as a commercial artist in his early years and enjoyed playing tricks with optical illusions, but Op Art proper grew out of a sustained and serious artistic project that he embarked on in the 1940s. His was a moral, Utopian vision: he hoped to bring beauty to all by developing a style of art that could be produced by ordinary workers, even machines. The artist would lose the privileged position hitherto reserved for genius, and not just because production would be taken out of his or her hands. Works of the kind that Vasarely was envisaging, relying as they did on the participation of the perceiving brain for their completion, would effectively make viewers the creators of the works they saw.

CREATED

Aix-en-Provence, France

MEDIUM

Oil on canvas

PERIOD/SERIES/MOVEMENT

Op Art

SIMILAR WORKS

Richard Anuszkiewicz, *Diamond Chroma*, 1965

Victor Vasarely *Born* 1908 Pècs, Hungary

Died 1997

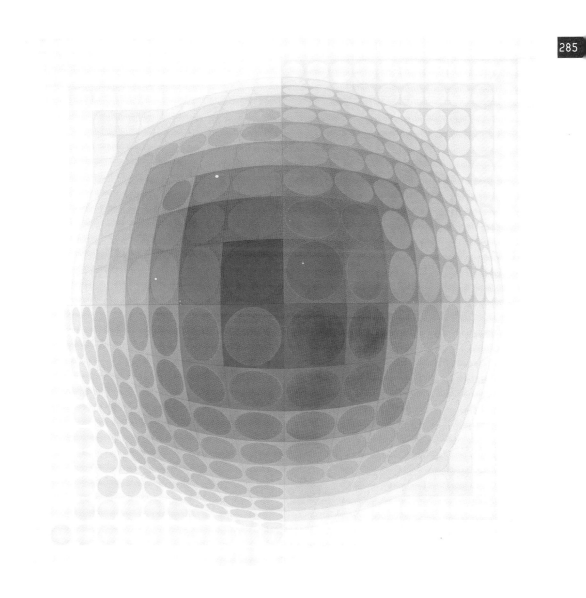

Riley, Bridget
Untitled (Nineteen Greys C), 1968

Courtesy of Private Collection/www.bridgeman.co.uk/© the artist

If to begin with, as we have seen, Op Art was connected to Pop by nothing stronger than a pun, that situation was very quickly – and comprehensively – to change. The appeal is not difficult to understand: the 'tricks' they play on the viewer are as entertaining as they are intriguing, the shimmering effects they produce often ravishing. Op effects were taken up with great enthusiasm and soon flooded the fields of popular design, featuring on everything from greetings cards to bathroom tiles and fashion fabrics. It should be noted, however, that Bridget Riley objected strongly to the plagiarism of her work, and sued the offending designers the length and breadth of Europe.

Bridget Riley's creations really caught the public imagination, and her art is immediately familiar through innumerable imitations. Yet, like Vasarely, Riley has always been engaged in a highly serious aesthetic project, exploring the part perception plays in the creation of beauty. The sense of three-dimensionality in a work like this one is at once irresistible and yet obviously illusory: we ourselves confer shape and form on what we know to be a flat canvas with a simple pattern, seeing distance in the 'fading' of the dots above and to either side.

CREATED

London

MEDIUM & DIMENSIONS

Screen print on card, 76.2 × 76.2 cm, Edition of 75

PERIOD/SERIES/MOVEMENT

Op Art

SIMILAR WORKS

François Morellet, *Geometree No. 51*, 1984

Larry Poons, *Via Regia*, 1964

Noland, Kenneth

Half, 1959

Kenneth Noland's work falls very roughly into the category of 'Abstract Expressionism', but this was a label with which, like several others of his generation, he was increasingly impatient: engrossing as they were, the works of painters such as Rothko and De Kooning appeared to them to seduce the viewer with a vision of transcendence that they repudiated. The 'soak-stain' works of Helen Frankenthaler were one way of taking the sense of artistic gesture and painterly texture out of the painted surface, and the poured 'veils' of Noland's friend Morris Louis (1912–62) were another. By 1959 Noland himself had embarked on a series of 'target' paintings in which, again, interest was focused on an impersonal surface.

In the course of the next few years Noland would refine these works, removing the rough edges and textures that seemed to him to hint at a meaning, a dimension beyond. The ideal of such 'Hard-Edge' art, as it was known, was to make each work a self-sealing entity, making closure with the canvas where it began and ended. 'What you see is what you see', as Frank Stella would remark.

CREATED

Washington, D.C.

MEDIUM

Acrylic on canvas

PERIOD/SERIES/MOVEMENT

Post-painterly Abstraction/Hard-Edge Painting/Green Mountain Boys

SIMILAR WORKS

Morris Louis, *Dalet Zayin*, 1959

Kenneth Noland *Born* 1924 Asheville, NC, USA

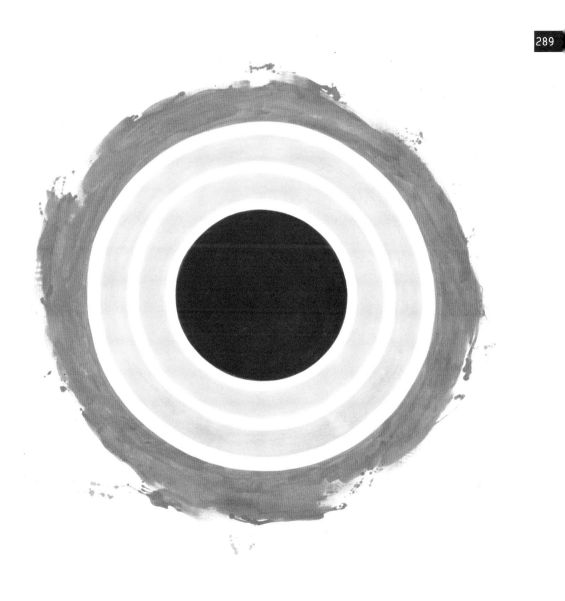

Kelly, Ellsworth
Blue Red, 1964

Courtesy of The Detroit Institute of Arts, USA, Founders Society Purchase, W. Hawkins Ferry Fund/www.bridgeman.co.uk/© Ellsworth Kelly

Many of those younger American artists generally grouped together with the 'Abstract Expressionists' of the 1940s and 1950s had actually made it their conscious objective to be as un-expressive as they could. This had been the mark at which Kenneth Noland's 'target' paintings had been aimed, and it was also the rationale behind the art of Ellsworth Kelly. 'High' Abstract Expressionism, they felt, showed too much of the individual creative consciousness and hinted at transcendent emotion and significance. This was no business of art they felt, a picture should simply be, and the viewer should enjoy it for what it is.

Kelly's 'Hard-Edge' paintings are hard in the sense that they present an impenetrable barrier to the view: there is no meaning or feeling there, nothing for the viewer to see through to. Where true Abstract Expressionist works resonate with emotion and inarticulate significance, here we have the picture and nothing more. This is to put things very negatively, of course, describing all the things such paintings lack. What they do have, something a whole generation of artists strove unceasingly for, is a sense of complete artistic self-containment and integrity.

CREATED

New York

MEDIUM & DIMENSIONS

Oil on canvas, 184.2 × 147.3 cm/72$\frac{1}{2}$ × 58 inches, EK 333

PERIOD/SERIES/MOVEMENT

Post-painterly Abstraction/Hard-Edge Painting

SIMILAR WORKS

Ad Reinhardt, *Abstract Painting*, 1960–66

Ellsworth Kelly *Born* 1923 Newburgh, NY, USA

Olitski, Jules
Non-Stop, 1965

Jules Olitski once remarked that his ideal painting would not even have a canvas to hold it but be 'nothing but some colours sprayed into the air and staying there'. At their best his works achieve something of the same effect. If one were to seek a word to describe their essential quality it might be 'haunting', or perhaps 'evocative', yet neither sits well with the intention of his work. His is not a romantic mistiness, but a colour cloud that the viewer wanders in without penetrating: it holds up the gaze as surely as the Hard-Edge wall.

Brought to America in infancy, Olitski enlisted in the Abstract Expressionist cause in the early 1950s, but like others found himself hankering after an art that would be less rich in associations and clearer in its own integrity. Like Helen Frankenthaler he enjoyed the play of different colours across a flat surface from which all sense of artistic gesture had been removed. He too experimented with 'soak-stain' techniques (see page 138) before, from the mid-1960s, beginning to use a spray gun to apply paint.

CREATED

New York

MEDIUM

Acrylic on canvas

PERIOD/SERIES/MOVEMENT

Post-painterly Abstraction/Green Mountain Boys

SIMILAR WORKS

Morris Louis, *Saraband*, 1959

Helen Frankenthaler, *Wales*, 1966

Jules Olitski *Born* 1922 Snovsk, Ukraine, Russia

Albers, Josef
Homage, 1954

Josef Albers taught at the Bauhaus before the Nazis closed it down in 1933, whereupon he and his wife Anni went to the United States as refugees. Both became teachers at North Carolina's famous Black Mountain College where they brought the skills and insights of the Bauhaus to a generation of young American artists. In 1950 Josef became head of the design department at Yale University – he was a distinguished academic, producing notable works on colour theory.

All this time he remained a working artist too, devoting himself to a long series of paintings collectively titled 'Homage to the Square'. This shape was particularly worthy of reverence, he felt, because exemplifying the ultimate in flatness and regularity it was the most quintessentially artificial, and thus artistic, of forms, the farthest possible from nature. Typically, as here, he set squares within one another, their subtly differentiated shades and tones creating distortions in apparent size. This aspect of his work offers parallels with some of the work being done by the Op Artists, one of whom, Richard Anuszkiewicz (b. 1930), was a student of his.

CREATED

New Haven, CT

MEDIUM

Oil on canvas

PERIOD/SERIES/MOVEMENT

Bauhaus/Op Art

SIMILAR WORKS

Richard Anuszkiewicz, *Trolley-Stop Still Life*, 1952

Josef Albers *Born* 1888 Westphalia, Germany

Died 1976

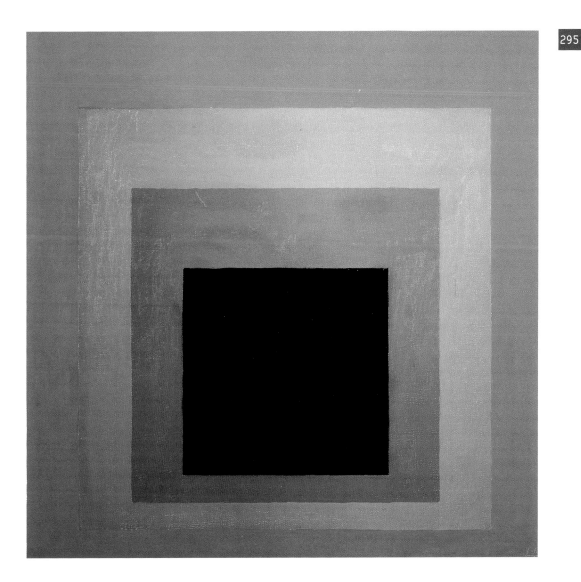

Stella, Frank
Agbatana II, 1968

There is a clear echo of Kenneth Noland's 'target' paintings in this work. Stella shared many of the older artist's preoccupations, yet over time the ways in which he would explore them would vary greatly. Even so an interest in geometrical forms remained more or less a constant, running through his works from the austere black-and-white 'pinstripe' paintings of the early 1960s to this work of almost carnival colour and humour.

Stella said his use of regular patterns helped him solve 'the painterly problems of what to put here and there and how to do it to make it go with what was there'. The remark was characteristically self-deprecatory, as he is up to dealing with most 'painterly problems' he is likely to encounter, but it chimes in with his wider approach to painting. In the spirit of the Hard-Edge school, Stella is in artistic principle uninterested in solving such problems: he wants his works to stand impersonal, self-contained. 'A good pictorial idea is worth more than a lot of manual dexterity', he maintains – the point of a painting is that it should be an idea embodied.

CREATED

New York

MEDIUM

Oil on canvas

PERIOD/SERIES/MOVEMENT

Post-painterly Abstraction/Hard-Edge Painting

SIMILAR WORKS

Al Held, *Hidden Fortress*, 1961

Kenneth Noland, *Drought*, 1962

Frank Stella *Born* 1936 Malden, Mass, USA

Richter, Gerhard

Abstract Painting, 1992

Every artist's life is an odyssey, perhaps, but Gerhard Richter has travelled farther than most, even if geographically he has simply moved from the east to the west of Germany. One of Europe's most beautiful cities, Richter's native Dresden, was flattened by Allied bombing in the Second World War, after which it belonged to the Communist German Democratic Republic.

Enormously talented but incorrigibly wayward, Richter was never cut out for the creation of Socialist-Realist icons, but his experiences gave him a strong sense of detachment towards artistic developments in the west. With his friend and fellow mischief maker Sigmar Polke (b. 1941), he established his own movement, Capitalist Realism, which called down a satirical plague on both Cold War houses. This was to be only the first in an ever-changing series of artistic postures in which Richter, by now a professional misfit, would apparently enlist in some school then get its values just slightly wrong. Hence we have had his out-of-focus Photorealism and, more recently, his Neo-Expressionist works. Characteristically Richter has prevaricated over whether he actually intends his work in this genre seriously or whether it has simply been another ironic pose.

CREATED

Cologne

MEDIUM

Oil on canvas

PERIOD/SERIES/MOVEMENT

Neo-Expressionism

SIMILAR WORKS

Sigmar Polke, *Magnetic Landscape*, 1982

Gerhard Richter *Born* 1932 Dresden, Germany

Kiefer, Anselm
Wolundlied, 1982

This evocation of the song of the mythical blacksmith, Wayland Smith, who was also king of the Elves according to European folklore, is characteristically apocalyptic. Within living memory of Nazism, Kiefer's treatment of national themes has caused some discomfort in his native Germany. He started out in Conceptual Art, and early images included photos of himself giving the Nazi salute, his mischief matching Gerhard Richter's and Sigmar Polke's. As a painter he has proved less utterly outrageous but still quite controversial enough, with a slightly gammy gothic quality to his references to the recent past. Despite this, Kiefer is much more than a prankster and indeed it has been his mischievous waywardness that has allowed him to attain true seriousness. Only someone of his bold irreverence could have attempted his sweeping artistic re-envisaging of the German story, rushing into historical realms were angels have for decades feared to tread. For critic Robert Hughes, Kiefer's is a project of the utmost importance, shaming that of most artists of the time. His work, he says, 'sets its face against the sterile irony, the despair of saying anything authentic about history or memory in paint ... It affirms the moral imagination'.

CREATED

Ornbach, Germany

MEDIUM

Oil on canvas

PERIOD/SERIES/MOVEMENT

Neo-Expressionism

SIMILAR WORKS

Georg Baselitz, *The Lamentation*, 1983

Anselm Kiefer *Born* 1945 Donaueschingen, Germany

Frost, Terry
Orchard Tambourines, 1999

Terry Frost is regarded as one of postwar Britain's most important abstract painters, though he himself didn't see it quite that way. He set out in his works to depict what he regarded as real scenes. Rather than reproduce the sights before him, however, he sought to capture the 'total experience' of the beholder, emotions and all. 'What I have painted', he said of one work, 'is an arrangement of form and colour that evokes for me a particular feeling.'

Hence the comparison with Abstract Expressionism, which was emerging in the United States at the same time as Frost's artistic career was taking shape at St Ives in the late 1940s and early 1950s. Critic Peter Fuller has suggested that the stars of the American movement drew unacknowledged inspiration from the St Ives School: that claim is controversial, to say the least. It does, however, highlight similarities of preoccupation and technique that can make comparisons between the two as interesting as they are potentially provocative. With its bright and boldly contrasting colours, its regular forms and its unapologetic flatness, this late woodcut has a cheery, even festive air.

CREATED

Newlyn, Cornwall

MEDIUM

Woodcut print

PERIOD/SERIES/MOVEMENT

Abstract Expressionism/St Ives School

SIMILAR WORKS

Peter Lanyon, *Coast*, 1953

Terry Frost *Born* 1915 Leamington Spa, England

Died 2003

Modern Art

Sculpture & 3D

Boccioni, Umberto
Unique Forms of Continuity in Space, 1913

Given the Futurist rage to explode the old artistic certainties of inert contour and solid mass, it is perhaps no surprise that they took little interest in sculpture. Yet Boccioni saw the apparently unpromising discipline as a fascinating challenge. Everywhere one looked in Europe's cities, he said, was 'a spectacle of such pitiable barbarism, clumsiness and monotonous imitation that my Futurist eye recoils from it in disgust'. Could Futurism do better? There was, Boccioni believed, 'a double cowardice of tradition and facility', which mired modern sculpture in mediocrity. Works were mere imitations of mere imitations: a Futurist sculpture would have to break this vicious circle. To do this, the inherited knowledge and 'expertise' of centuries would have to be jettisoned and the whole discipline reinvented. Underlying this, of course, was a more familiar Modernist message, and Boccioni's exhortations to abandon the external 'closed-form statue' and 'tear open the body' would have struck a chord with the Cubists in particular. Yet the striking dynamism and drama of his own works suggest he had identified a real artistic opportunity, which other Futurists might profitably have explored.

CREATED

Milan

MEDIUM

Bronze

PERIOD/SERIES/MOVEMENT

Futurism

SIMILAR WORKS

Henri Gaudier-Brzeska, *Birds Erect*, 1914

Umberto Boccioni *Born* 1882 Reggio Calabria, Italy

Died 1916

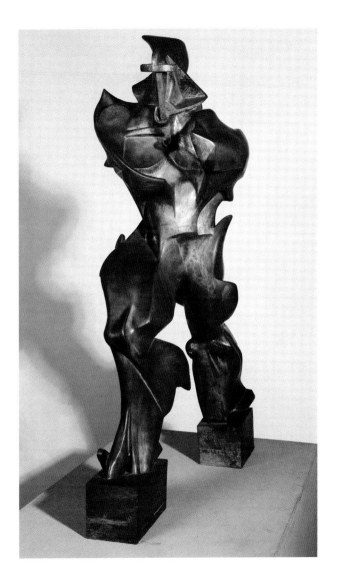

Gaudier-Brzeska, Henri

Mermaid, 1912–13

Henri Gaudier-Brzeska is generally categorized as a 'Vorticist' and was indeed an outspoken advocate of Percy Wyndham Lewis's (1882–1957) cause, but figures like this one show just how varied his work could be. The sleeping mermaid here shows a hint of Primitivism – a common if paradoxical preoccupation among Modernists – but none of the jagged lines and tortured forms that are associated with Vorticism. Some of Gaudier-Brzeska's other sculptures certainly do display such features (see, for instance, *Redstone Dancer*, 1913). Much of his work, however, harks back to the older tradition in which he was trained, remembering the nineteenth-century style of Rodin.

A Frenchman living in London, Gaudier-Brzeska was inevitably a man of overlapping loyalties. He was one of the founders of the 'London Group'. Not to be confused with the 'School of London' dating from the 1940s, the 'London Group' was formed in 1913. Its young members resented the influence of the Royal Academy and, since one of its aims was to open up an insular English artworld to continental ideas, Gaudier-Brzeska was able to play a crucial role.

CREATED

London

MEDIUM

Bronze

PERIOD/SERIES/MOVEMENT

Vorticism

SIMILAR WORKS

Jacob Epstein, *Doves (First Version)*, 1913

Henri Gaudier-Brzeska *Born* 1891 near Orleans, France

Died 1915

Man Ray

Metronome (Object to be Destroyed), 1923–72

'Cut out the eye from a photograph of one who has been loved but is seen no more. Attach the eye to the pendulum of a metronome and set the weight to the tempo required. Keep going to the limit of endurance. With a hammer well-aimed, try to destroy the whole with a single blow.' Despite these words, this famous artwork does not seem to have been destroyed; on the contrary, it was re-made repeatedly over decades after its first creation in 1923.

It is significant that Man Ray's comments do not take the form of a description, rather they are instructions for assembly. While he clearly envisages an unsettlingly personal relationship between bereft viewer and beloved as they watch each other watching, he also saw this work as infinitely reproducible and ultimately disposable. In this respect the American Dadaist and Surrealist can be seen to be anticipating the values of Pop Art: his was indeed an extremely broad and extraordinarily far-seeing creative mind. A photographer, a painter, a draughtsman, film maker and sculptor, he made an incalculable contribution across the whole spectrum of twentieth-century art.

CREATED

Paris/New York

MEDIUM

Wood, metal and paper

PERIOD/SERIES/MOVEMENT

Dada/Surrealism

SIMILAR WORKS

Marcel Duchamp, *Bicycle Wheel*, 1951, third version, after lost original of 1913

Man Ray (born Emmanuel Radinski) *Born* 1890 Philadelphia, USA

Died 1976

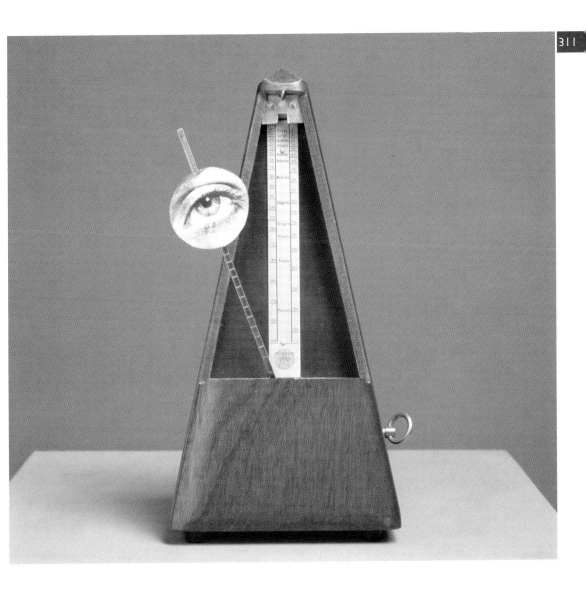

Schlemmer, Oskar

Ornamentale Plastik, 1919

This work was actually created the year before Schlemmer took up his teaching position at the Bauhaus, but goes far to explain why Walter Gropius (1883–1969) was so eager to give his students the benefits of Schlemmer's skills. While clearly a work of resolute abstraction, it incorporates suggestions of a ship's ventilator funnels and organ pipes, which hint at the achievements of human industry and art. Such symbolism was thoroughly in keeping with Gropius's declared ambition to bring together the spheres of art and industry and produce a new aesthetic of beautiful functionalism for modern life.

Just how broadly the Bauhaus defined the role of art is evident from Schlemmer's teaching of life classes there from 1926. His course, Der Mensch ('Man') was part of the syllabus of the theatre workshop at the Bauhaus. The human figure was always at the centre of his ideas, works and writings, and the more he taught at the Bauhaus, the more he emphasised the role of man, the human figure. This presents an interesting paradox. If the Bauhaus had survived the Nazis, it might well have run up against the limitations of the new, modern age: how comfortably could art and industry really get along?

CREATED

Stuttgart

MEDIUM

Plaster

PERIOD/SERIES/MOVEMENT

Bauhaus

SIMILAR WORKS

Otto Werner, *Architectural Sculpture,* 1922

Oskar Schlemmer *Born* 1888 Stuttgart, Germany

Died 1943

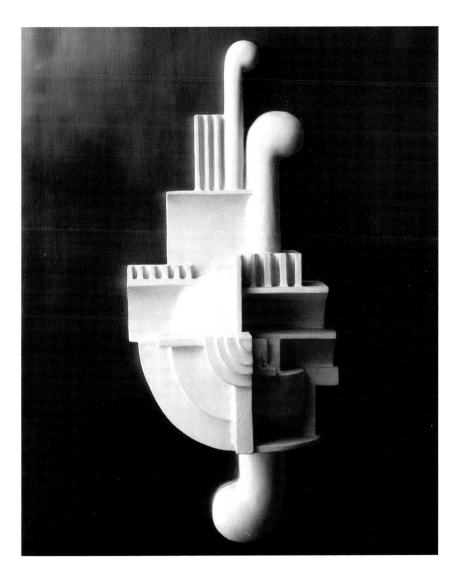

Brancusi, Constantin
Mademoiselle Pogani, c. 1920

'They are imbeciles who call my work abstract', wrote Constantin Brancusi. 'That which they call abstract is the most realist, because what is real is not the exterior form but the idea, the essence of things.' The position is a combative one, yet at bottom Brancusi's view is strikingly similar to that expressed by the other great practitioners of twentieth-century Abstract art.

His work is at once primitive and perfect. Much influenced by the folk art of Africa and his native Romania, Brancusi was fully schooled in the tradition of sculpture that followed Rodin. He rebelled against the French master, however, most obviously in his tendency towards abstraction but more profoundly in his sheer perfectionism. So suggests the contemporary British sculptor William Tucker: 'Rodin, the modeller, is the sculptor as *initiator*: his sculpture has the energy of beginning, the first touch; ... Brancusi took carving to be the reverse of this process: his is the last hand to touch the object; he is the sculptor as finisher.'

CREATED

Paris

MEDIUM

Bronze

PERIOD/SERIES/MOVEMENT

École de Paris

SIMILAR WORKS

Henri Gaudier-Brzeska, *Maternity*, 1913

Jacob Epstein, *Ecce Homo*, 1934–35

Constantin Brancusi *Born* 1876 Hobitza, Romania

Died 1957

Arp, Jean Hans
Hybrid Fruit Called Pagoda, 1935

Jean Arp was one of several Dadaists who drifted into Surrealism, though the two movements were not as similar as they may immediately seem. Dada rejoiced in nonsense for its own sake; Surrealism pursued absurdity as a means to the end of uncovering the deeper logic of the subconscious and of dream. There was a sense, then, in which Surrealism set out to be 'realistic', however irrational the reality it recorded. It is striking that several painters of the school excelled in meticulous, quasi-realist representational work – Salvador Dalí (1904–89), for example.

In a similar spirit, Jean Arp approached his later Abstract sculptures as though they were figurative depictions of natural forms, but of natural forms that had never actually existed. 'I tried to make forms grow', he said. 'I put my trust in the example of seeds, stars, clouds, plants, animals, men, and finally in my innermost being.' Arp created other important works across a range of different genres, but these organic sculptures seem likely to prove the most enduring. In their sheer simplicity and sensuousness, they are just as striking today as when they were first created in the 1930s.

CREATED

Meudon, near Paris

MEDIUM

Bronze

PERIOD/SERIES/MOVEMENT

Dada/Surrealism

SIMILAR WORKS

Max Ernst, *The King Playing with his Queen*, 1944

Jean (Hans) Arp *Born* 1886 Strasbourg, France

Died 1966

Giacometti, Alberto

Woman with her Throat Cut, 1932

Surrealist art is often fun. Drawing as it does on dream and the subconscious, it makes the strangest connections, and juxtaposes the unlikeliest images. But dreams may easily be nightmares – the struggle of the civilized ego to control the primitive drives of the subconscious id (in Sigmund Freud's famous terms) articulates itself in all manner of unresolved anxieties, unacknowledged terrors and violent desires. The very title of Giacometti's *Woman with her Throat Cut* is shocking; as for the sculpture itself, that is harrowing on a number of different levels. From the gaunt, dehumanized stick-insect body to the sprung tautness in its spread-eagled position, what should be a limp corpse seems charged with the suggestion of violence. What does the woman symbolize here? Is she victim or attacker? Her image threatens rather than evoking sympathy. Giacometti came into vogue in the postwar period, when his skeletal figures were held to suggest the figures of those confined in the death camps of Nazi Germany. However, that same basic figural style and that same preoccupation with violence had been features of his work since long before.

CREATED

Paris

MEDIUM

Bronze

PERIOD/SERIES/MOVEMENT

Surrealism

SIMILAR WORKS

Joan Miró, *Woman with Fine Breasts*, 1969

Alberto Giacometti *Born* 1901 Borgonovo, Switzerland

Died 1966

Dalí, Salvador

Telephone-Homard, 1936

André Breton kept his Surrealist followers on a tight artistic leash, conducting himself like a commissar. For some time his movement was actually affiliated to the French Communist Party, which in the 1920s made perfect sense. First, Communism represented the future: the Russian Revolution had been the most exciting political event in generations and the Soviet Union was yet to discredit itself completely. Second, more theoretically, there was a clear analogy between the Marxist view that the evolving economic structures of society determined the way its cultural structures developed and the relationship between the subconscious and conscious minds in psychoanalytic theory. Before long the movement had its dissidents, the most famous being Salvador Dali, a man whose contrariness was as awesome as his talent. He made no secret of his political conservatism but was aesthetically wayward too. For Dali, it soon became clear that Surrealism was not an all-embracing ideology but an interesting artistic idea and visual vocabulary to be explored. He loved to surprise, to outrage, and to exercise his extraordinary imagination and irreverent wit in works such as this wonderfully whimsical lobster telephone.

CREATED

Paris

MEDIUM

Plastic, painted plaster and mixed media

PERIOD/SERIES/MOVEMENT

Surrealism

SIMILAR WORKS

Max Ernst, *Lunar Asparagus*, 1935

Salvador Dalí *Born* 1936 Figueras, Spain

Died 1989

Hepworth, Barbara
Figure (Archaean), 1959

Barbara Hepworth's sculptures have the air of having grown spontaneously out of the ground, perhaps because she found inspiration in the landscape of her longtime Cornish home. There were other influences as well: several artists had developed similar interests at about the same time, including Jean Arp on the Continent and Henry Moore in England. Hepworth's creations nevertheless remain utterly individual in their monumental dignity and in their fidelity to the media in which she worked. 'I do not want to make a stone horse that is trying to and cannot smell the air,' she insisted, 'but to make exactly the right relation of masses, a living thing in stone, to express my awareness and thought of these things.' Her medium, then, was her subject. She had a mystic sense of its essential character and its relation to her as artist and to the world.

Her introduction of the 'hole' in her sculptures was controversial at first, but again reflects her desire to get to the heart of things. Revealing the tension between inner core and outer surface, it recalls Boccioni's cry for a sculpture that would 'tear open the body'.

CREATED

St Ives, Cornwall

MEDIUM

Embossed bronze

PERIOD/SERIES/MOVEMENTZ

Organic Abstraction/St Ives School/Unit One

SIMILAR WORKS

Jean Arp, *Sculpture of Silence*, 1930–31

Barbara Hepworth *Born* 1903 Wakefield, England

Died 1975

Moore, Henry

Reclining Figure: Festival, edition of 5, 1951

As a promising young sculptor in 1930, Henry Moore was calling on his contemporaries to remove the 'Greek spectacles' from their eyes. Like Barbara Hepworth, he believed the spirit of the earth, the material and the medium were everything: 'Stone', he firmly insisted, 'should look like stone ... The sculpture which moves me most', he went on, 'is full-blooded and self-supporting, fully in the round ... it is not perfectly symmetrical, it is static and it is strong and vital, giving out something of the energy and power of great mountains. It has a life of its own, independent of the object it represents.'

By the time he came to create this figure for the Festival of Britain he was arguably England's most famous artist, but the same values continued to inform his work. In keeping with their elemental mysticism, both he and Hepworth had long preferred to work in stone, hewing out shapes by what they called 'direct carving'. Eventually they would come to find the flexibility of work in bronze just as satisfying in its different way.

CREATED

London

MEDIUM

Bronze

PERIOD/SERIES/MOVEMENT

Organic Abstraction/Unit One

SIMILAR WORKS

Joan Miró, *Lunar Bird*, 1944–46, enlarged and cast, 1966–67

Henry Spencer Moore *Born* 1898 Castleford, England

Died 1986

Tinguely, Jean & Rivers, Larry

Turning of Friendship of America and France, 1961

'Le Mouvement' was the punning title of the first-ever exhibition of kinetic art in 1955 – these were works that moved, not emotionally but literally. Several participating artists, including Yaacov Agam (b. 1928) and Jesús Raphael Soto (b. 1923), were later to find fame with the craze for Op Art. Already, however, they were exploring the place of perception in the artistic experience.

Whether moved by a motor, by magnetism or simply by the breeze in an outdoor setting, a piece of kinetic art was never static. That in itself set it apart from more traditional works, but there was another difference too. Movement meant change and ever-shifting perspective, thus the viewer would never see precisely the same image twice: therefore how far could they feel they were viewing a single work of art? So much for the theory: kinetic art worked because it was pleasing to look at. Jean Tinguely's art works because it is so full of wit and humour. Arguably his contraptions send up the high-flown theory, a tendency that was to reach its logical conclusion in his 'auto-destructive' machines.

CREATED

New York

MEDIUM

Mixed media

PERIOD/SERIES/MOVEMENT

Kinetic Art

SIMILAR WORKS

Kenneth Snelson, *Needle Tower*, 1968

Jean Tinguely *Born* 1925 Fribourg, Switzerland

Died 1991

Larry Rivers *Born* 1923 New York, USA

Died 2002

Calder, Alexander

Twisty Beast, 1970

It has the look of a Miró painting in three dimensions (something Miró sculpture seldom does), but it was Calder's declared ambition to paint 'moving Mondrians'. Like Ben Nicholson – but to very different ends – he had been bowled over by the experience of a visit to the Dutch master's Paris studio and determined to develop his own, animated version of *De Stijl*. The pure colours of the sails on this mobile from 1970 are an obvious allusion to Piet Mondrian's (1872–1944) work. Miró's influence is apparent too (although less than in many other Calder mobiles) in the use of vaguely 'biomorphic' shapes, forms that have the character of living, growing organisms.

This was key to kinetic art as envisaged by Alexander Calder, with movement conferring an all-important element of life on a composition. Additionally, since the mobile changed as it went round, from a perceptual point of view at least, it registered the passage of time as the conventionally 'timeless' artwork clearly never could.

CREATED

Paris/New York

MEDIUM

Standing mobile, painted sheet metal and wire

PERIOD/SERIES/MOVEMENT

Kinetic Art

SIMILAR WORKS

László Moholy-Nagy, *Light-Space Modulator*, 1930

Takis, *Aeolian Olympic Rings*, 2004

Alexander Calder *Born* 1898 Lawnton, PA, USA

Died 1976

Arman

Tamerlane's Memorial, 1961

In the fourteenth century the Tartar warlord Tamerlane blazed a trail of destruction across Central Asia and into the Middle East, piling up pyramids of his enemies' skulls wherever he went. The French-born artist Arman makes macabre play with this story in one of his famous 'accumulations'. Armand created this work on the eve of his departure for New York, and since that time he has become known as an American artist. He was formed in France, however, coming of age as part of the Nouveau Réalisme movement that was founded by Pierre Restany and Yves Klein. Armand was fascinated and appalled by the ways of consumerism.

While this work obviously looks back to the horrors of history, and – we see now – forward to the evils of regimes like that of Cambodia's Pol Pot, its main subject is the wastage of everyday Western life, and what it might mean. 'I didn't discover the principle of "accumulation",' Armand said, 'It discovered me. It has always been obvious that society feeds its sense of security with a pack-rat instinct demonstrated in its window displays, its assembly lines, its garbage piles.'

CREATED

Paris

MEDIUM

Mixed media

PERIOD/SERIES/MOVEMENT

Nouveau Réalisme ('New Realism')

SIMILAR WORKS

César, *Compression*, 1960

Mimmo Rotella, *From Sicily*, 1961

Arman (born Armand Fernandez) *Born* 1928 Nice, France

Christo

Package, 1959

Courtesy of Musée Cantini, Marseilles, France, Giraudon/www.bridgeman.co.uk/© Christo

In their attempts to re-imagine Realism, artists of the early 1960s made a variety of different interventions in the actual environment. Arman's 'accumulations' are a good example; so too would be César's 'compressions' (bales of mechanically crushed scrap metal) and the reverse collage (torn posters, for example) of Raymond Hains and Mimmo Rotella. While it would be wrong to regard Nouveau Réalisme as the origin of Installation Art (the indefatigable Marcel Duchamp created his *Mile of String* in New York, 1942), the movement had emphatically focused attention on the meeting point of artist and environment.

That this would lead almost inevitably to installation is clear from the career of Christo and Jeanne-Claude, now known for closing off streets and wrapping up public buildings around the world. The relationship of this work with its viewer and its world is very different: what is displayed here is concealment itself; an implied object (who knows what, if anything?) has been covered up by the intervention of the artist.

CREATED

Paris

MEDIUM

Rope and fabric

PERIOD/SERIES/MOVEMENT

Installation Art

SIMILAR WORKS

Niki de Saint-Phalle, *Gorgo in New York*, 1962

César, *Compression Mobil*, 1960

Christo (born Christo Vladimirov Javacheff) *Born* 1935 Gabrovno, Bulgaria

Nevelson, Louise

Tropical Garden II, 1959

It has the look of a stately sculpted frieze, or some Babylonian bas-relief – this work would not have been out of place in some ancient palace or temple. In fact it was put together from odds and ends of wood picked up from New York's streets in the artist's nightly scavenging expeditions. Louise Nevelson was living in poverty and materials were expensive: necessity was the mother of this invention. It made artistic sense too. Since the days of Dada, artists such as Kurt Schwitters (1887–1948) and Marcel Duchamp (1887–1968) had been experimenting with 'readymades' and *objets trouvés* ('found objects'). The Dadaists loved the sheer serendipity of Assemblage Art, the nonsensical juxtapositions it allowed to be made; yet Nevelson had other inspirations. She had leftist sympathies and had worked with Ben Shahn (1898–1969) as assistant to Diego Rivera (1886–1957) on his ill-fated Rockefeller Center mural (see page 194).

On the face of it Nevelson's art could hardly be more different either from Shahn's Social-Realist works or the revolutionary panoramas of Rivera. Still, her creations clearly commemorate the heroism of the everyday, the nobility of ordinary Americans.

CREATED

New York

MEDIUM

Painted wood

PERIOD/SERIES/MOVEMENT

Assemblage

SIMILAR WORKS

Joseph Cornell, *Untitled (Grand Hôtel de l'Observatoire)*, 1954

Louise Nevelson (born Louise Berliawsky) *Born* 1899, Kiev, Russia

Died 1988

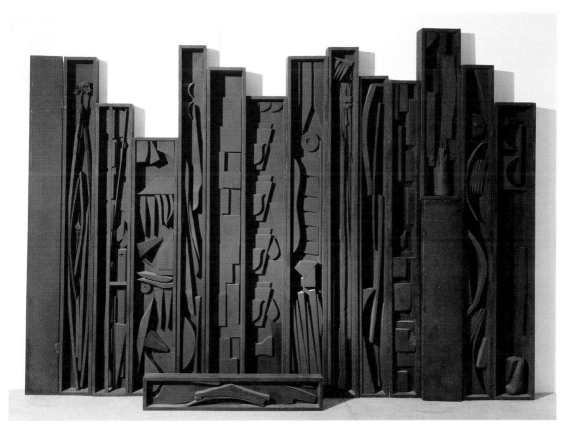

Oldenburg, Claes
Fried Egg in Pan, 1961

Pop Artists were fascinated by the interface between high art and the mass media, and the consumerism all that imagery represented. It was but a short leap from the labels of soup tins to, if not the soup itself, then other foodstuffs such as Oldenburg's fried eggs and foam-rubber hamburgers. It was but another short step from sending up the market culture to entering into its activities: Oldenburg even opened up his own 'store' in 1962. Such projects maintained a fastidious ironic distance from the grubby business of buying and selling in earnest, of course, but what had once been a gulf was narrowing all the time. With designers creating Pop furniture and other items that could be bought and installed in the affluent home, there was a danger (if that was how one looked at it, of course) of the distinction disappearing altogether.

Oldenburg is old-fashioned in this respect, as works such as *Lipstick Ascending on Caterpillar Tracks* (1969, Yale University Art Gallery) make clear: his concern was that art should not 'sit on its ass' but engage with the stuff of everyday existence.

CREATED
New York

MEDIUM & DIMENSIONS
Metal frying pan and plaster painted with enamel, 9.2 x 39.4 x 20 cm/3⅝ x 15½ x 7⅞ inches

PERIOD/SERIES/MOVEMENT
Pop Art

SIMILAR WORKS
George Segal, *The Parking Garage*, 1968

Claes Oldenburg *Born* 1929 Stockholm, Sweden

Rauschenberg, Robert
Bed, 1955

The quintessential work of 'Combine Painting', *Bed* very nearly never happened, and that provision is part of its enduring charm. Rauschenberg only thought of using his bed linen, he says, because he had run out of conventional canvas, but he could not have hit upon a more apt vehicle for his imagination. The resulting image is rich in often-contradictory resonances. On the one hand the bed suggests comfort (Rauschenberg has expressed the fear that someone will be tempted to tuck themselves up in it); on the other, for some it has suggested a murder scene. *Bed* is also ambiguously situated between painting and sculpture. In some ways it looks forward to the installations of the 1990s and beyond, but at the same time the paintwork is in the spirit of an Abstract Expressionism, which was by then very much the artistic style of the establishment.

From today's stand point the stylistic paradoxes are still more evident: viewed through the prism of Pop we register an interest in repetition à la Warhol. Yet the patchwork squares that create this effect represent an art form of a particularly old-fashioned and parochial sort, the ultimate symbol of homely American domesticity.

CREATED

New York

MEDIUM

Mixed media

PERIOD/SERIES/MOVEMENT

Pop Art/Neo-Dada/Combine Painting

SIMILAR WORKS

Tracey Emin, *My Bed*, 1998

Robert Rauschenberg   *Born* 1925 Port Arthur, TX, USA

Andre, Carl

Tomb of the Golden Engenderers, 1976

Carl Andre has his own little footnote in the cultural history of Great Britain as the man behind the notorious 'Tate Bricks'. *Equivalent VIII* was first displayed in 1976 to the outrage of the public, or rather the press. This was by no means the first work of art to cause an outcry, and by the last decade of the twentieth century such scandals had become more or less daily fare, but this furore was slightly different from most of those that had gone before. In the main what had offended previously in paintings, sculpture, novels or films had been what was regarded as obscene or improper content: material involving sex, violence, bad language, insults to racial groups or patriotic pride. Far from having improper content of this sort, Andre's work seemed to have no content at all – the complaint was that the 'Tate Bricks' were a waste of public money.

Artists disliked the 'Minimalist' tag, in fact, precisely because it did imply that something was missing in their works, when really – as perhaps this work shows more clearly – they sought to explore the same geometric and spatial territory as the Constructivists and, in particular, the Suprematists.

CREATED

New York

MEDIUM

Western red cedar wood

PERIOD/SERIES/MOVEMENT

Minimalism

SIMILAR WORKS

Robert Morris, *Untitled (Corner Piece)*, 1964

Carl Andre *Born* 1935 Quincy, MA, USA

Flavin, Dan

Untitled (To Agrati), 1964

The debt of Minimalism to early twentieth-century Russian models is obvious. However, also evident in a work such as this one by Dan Flavin is its kinship with the Post-painterly Abstraction with which it was contemporaneous. This work in particular recalls Helen Frankenthaler's (b. 1928) 'soak-stain' paintings (see page 138) and the sprayed paintings of Jules Olitski (see page 294). The light may be soft and a little eerie, yet this is still a recognizably 'Hard-Edged' work in that it resists reading, offering no hint of significance or spiritual content in its simplicity.

Post-painterly Abstraction set no store by the individual gesture or touch of the creating artist, hence the poured 'veils' of Morris Louis or Frank Stella's disavowals of technique. Minimalist sculpture, too, makes a virtue of impersonality. Flavin's work would fulfil its purpose no more successfully if he himself had made the fluorescent tubes that it comprises: he is happy to use industrially produced materials. The conception is everything; execution just a matter of assembly. This is abstraction at its very purest.

CREATED

New York

MEDIUM

Fluorescent tubes

PERIOD/SERIES/MOVEMENT

Minimalism

SIMILAR WORKS

Ellsworth Kelly, *Untitled*, 1986

Dan Flavin *Born* 1933 New York, USA

Died 1996

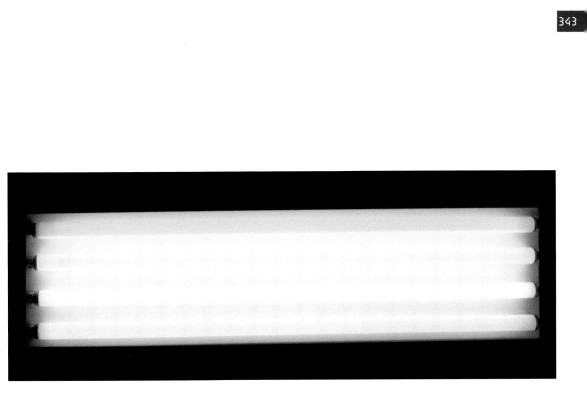

Judd, Donald
Untitled, 1969

Donald Judd did not see himself as a sculptor. He might well have been a painter, except that a painting was just 'a rectangular plane placed flat against the wall'. In 1965 in an article that came to be regarded as the unofficial manifesto of the Minimalist movement, he spelled out his objections both to painting and to sculpture as then conceived. Specificity was central, he felt, and that meant three dimensions – 'real space'. It also implied colour, something that sculpture conventionally lacked. His works would hang from the walls like paintings, but have sculptural specificity. They were also to have simplicity, of course, the fundamental virtue for Minimalist art, although it was the simplicity not of ignorance but of understanding stripped down to its absolute essentials. As Judd's fellow Minimalist, Robert Morris, put it, 'Simplicity of shape does not necessarily equate with simplicity of experience. Unitary forms do not reduce relationships. They order them'.

Such ideas seemed terribly elusive in the 1960s, but today they are a great deal easier to get hold of intuitively perhaps due to the fact that we live in a world that is more or less governed by binary computer code.

CREATED

New York

MEDIUM

Copper and fluorescent red Plexiglas

PERIOD/SERIES/MOVEMENT

Minimalism

SIMILAR WORKS

Eva Hesse, *Sans II*, 1968

Donald Judd *Born* 1928 Excelsior Springs, MO, USA

Died 1994

Tucker, William
Thebes, 1966

Courtesy of Arts Council Collection, Hayward Gallery, London, UK/www.bridgeman.co.uk/© William Tucker

A series of 'New Generation' exhibitions were mounted at the Whitechapel Gallery in London in the mid-1960s to present work by up-and-coming young British artists of the time. As is generally the case, a wide variety of work was featured – this might be a generation but it was not a coherent school. Despite this, those exhibiting at the 1965 show included a group of talented sculptors who did seem to belong together to some extent. Phillip King, Tim Scott, David Annesley and others were all artists of great individuality, yet common themes seemed to be emerging in their work.

Of all the 'New Generation' sculptors, William Tucker has probably proved the most enduringly successful down the decades, but his work of the mid-1960s was very recognizably a product of its time. *Thebes* has the bright colours and playfulness of Pop Art, the wave-like elements seem to have been let fall haphazardly and off-balance, but there is a Minimalist severity about it too. If the curved contours of the one face suggest the organic style of Hepworth or Moore, these are set against right-angled corners and flat sides.

CREATED

London

MEDIUM

Painted wood

PERIOD/SERIES/MOVEMENT

New Generation/Minimalism

SIMILAR WORKS

David Annesley, *Big Yellow Circle*, 1966

Phillip King, *Dunstable Reel*, 1970

William Tucker *Born* 1935 Cairo, Egypt

Beuys, Joseph
Earth Telephone, 1968

Joseph Beuys was a phenomenon. Not, perhaps, postwar Germany's greatest genius, but he was certainly among the most colourful characters on the postwar political, cultural and social scene. A pilot in the Luftwaffe, he had been shot down over the Eastern Front and taken in by Tartar nomads, he liked to claim. From them he had acquired special insights into their ancient shamanistic religion and a lifelong attachment to the rough materials of their existence: earth, fat and felt. A one-man counterculture, Beuys went on to embrace the 1960s and 1970s, staging sit-ins, happenings and outrageous Performance Art. For one he paraded up and down the galleries of Düsseldorf's art museum explaining the pictures to a dead hare; in another he called for the Berlin wall to be raised by 5 cm (2 in) and sparked off a student riot.

Here, perhaps, the shaman shows us his direct line into the earth, a witty play on the idea of being 'earthed' and rooted. It was also a swipe at German nationalism's traditional obsession with the idea of connecting with the soil.

CREATED

Düsseldorf

MEDIUM

Telephone, earth, grass and connecting cable on wooden board

PERIOD/SERIES/MOVEMENT

Conceptual Art

SIMILAR WORKS

John Baldessari, *Specimen (After Dürer)*, 2000

Joseph Beuys *Born* 1921 Krefeld, Germany

Died 1986

Manzoni, Piero
Merda d'Artista, 1961

This work is just what it says on the tin. Manzoni prepared and labelled 90 cans of his own excrement, numbered them as a prestigious limited edition and offered them for sale. He carefully calculated the price to equal the current rate for gold. So, was he being serious here or simply having a laugh? That question has arisen over and over with works of art ever since the days of Dada. Generally speaking, of course, the answer is 'both'. The joke is on the art world, which fosters the cult of the artist as genius, conferring such value on his basest excretions. At the same time, however, it treats him without regard, buying and selling his creations as though they were any other commodities.

More seriously Manzoni wants to exalt the body and its products, which he feels have been undervalued in western culture. Although the idealized nude has been displayed, physical corporeality has been a source only of embarrassment: Manzoni sets out to draw attention to this injustice. Previously he had blown up balloons, creating artworks with his breath; *Merda d'Artista* was an obvious next step.

CREATED

Milan

MEDIUM

Mixed media

PERIOD/SERIES/MOVEMENT

Conceptual Art

SIMILAR WORKS

Yves Klein, *Untitled Anthropometry (ANT 101)*, 1960

Piero Manzoni *Born* 1933 Soncino, Italy

Died 1963

PRODUCED BY

Piero Manzoni

N.°

Oppenheim, Dennis
Maze, 1970

The Great Serpent Mound goes snaking across some 400 m (1,300 ft) of rural Ohio, constructed by people of the Hopewell Culture over 1,500 years ago. Ritual earthworks of one sort or another were built a long time earlier in prehistoric times. Today we cannot begin to understand the social and cultural forces that motivated the construction of such monuments, but they still speak to us, or so at least it seems.

Sated with consumerist plenty, many have begun to look out across an earth exhausted by industrial exploitation and started to hanker after what were apparently simpler times. New Age spirituality has invested the earth with all manner of mystic forces, but even the most sceptical share something of the same nostalgia. Artists have been no exception: many have been motivated by quasi-religious feelings of this kind; others have simply seen the earth as a new space just waiting to be inscribed. There is general agreement, though, that they must 'work with' the earth, and a general rejection of the traditional paradigm that the landscape is a spirit to be broken, a 'wilderness' to be 'tamed'.

CREATED

Whitewater, WI

PERIOD/SERIES/MOVEMENT

Earth Art

SIMILAR WORKS

Christo and Jeanne-Claude, *Wrapped Coast, Little Bay, Australia*, 1969

Walter De Maria, *Lightning Field*, 1977

Dennis Oppenheim *Born* 1938 Mason City, WA, USA

Long, Richard

Cornish Stone Circle, 1978

Richard Long has been Britain's leading practitioner of Earth Art, attracting much attention with a range of works created both in the open landscape and in galleries. Oddly, on the face of it, he talks in terms of his sculptures not being built, but 'made by walking in landscapes'. His own experience of traversing the countryside is thus an integral part of his completed work.

This claim is a good deal easier to accept in practice in the presence of the works themselves, than it is to understand in theory: Long's creations are most wonderfully evocative. His is not a mumbo-jumbo mysticism: while he has forged a fascinating connection between contemporary and prehistoric sculptural forms, his love of the landscape is more obviously Romantic than explicitly spiritual. As much as anything, he is concerned to 'extend the boundaries of sculpture' and enable it to be 'deconstructed ... in space and time'. He is interested in human transience, in the marks we make on our environment, the monuments we build and the unwitting footprints we leave behind.

CREATED

England

MEDIUM

Stone

PERIOD/SERIES/MOVEMENT

Earth Art

SIMILAR WORKS

Robert Smithson, *Spiral Jetty*, 1970

Joseph Beuys, *The End of the Twentieth Century*, 1983–85

Richard Long *Born* 1945 Bristol, England

Merz, Mario
Mario Merz, 1988

Courtesy of Nationalgalerie, Berlin, Germany/Wolfgang Neeb/© Mario Merz

One of a series of 'igloos' created by Mario Merz, who seems originally to have envisaged them as emblematic dwelling places for a post-apocalyptic existence, but then to have moved gradually towards the realms of sci-fi. That progression, some say, is of a piece with what started out as a rebellious and anti-materialistic movement, which has made its peace, very profitably, with the established art world over time.

The name *Arte Provera* was first employed by curator and critic Germano Celant in the mid-1960s to describe the output of a group of artists who were working in northern Italy at that time. Their use of cast-off materials, such as rags (often set ironically against stylized, Classical forms) questioned the relationship of art to wealth, prestige and history. It was a stripped-down style, not in the formal way in which Minimalism was, but in the sense that it attempted to produce works that, while making contact with the past, would not be complicated by the accumulated associations of artistic tradition. Often, as here, such works were ultimately extravagantly conceived and expensive to create: this was *Arte Povera* only in a very notional sense.

MEDIUM

Mixed media

PERIOD/SERIES/MOVEMENT

Arte Povera ('Impoverished Art')

SIMILAR WORKS

Michelangelo Pistoletto, *Broken Mirror*, 1978

Giovanni Anselmo, *Grays Lightening Towards Ultramarine*, 1988

Mario Merz *Born* 1925 Milan, Italy

Kounellis, Jannis
Untitled, 1978

Courtesy of loan to the Hamburg Kunsthalle, Hamburg, Germany/www.bridgeman.co.uk/© Jannis Kounellis

Bound and gagged by the same cord, head and hair half sheared away, a broken Classical face gazes impassively at the viewer in this work by Kounellis. A native of Greece, Kounellis has spent just about his entire working life in Italy, the nation that gave the world its antiquity-inspired Renaissance.

Tradition weighs heavily upon Kounellis, as it has upon many Italian artists in recent years, hence the enthusiasm generated by the ideas of *Arte Povera*. This was as much a rejection of art tradition as it was of modern capitalism, although it was certainly imbued with the revolutionary 'Spirit of '68'. Kounellis's particular complaint was against the conventions that had come to define what constituted a work of art, and which governed the ways such works should be presented. These, he said, had ended up dictating what should have been the free development of art, creating 'an inertia of style'. Hence this image of an art enslaved, the figure mutilated, restricted and silenced by the sheer fact of being set on a plinth for exhibition in the gallery.

CREATED

Rome

MEDIUM

Plaster, body colour, cord, iron plinth

PERIOD/SERIES/MOVEMENT

Arte Povera ('Impoverished Art')

SIMILAR WORKS

Luciano Fabro, *Demeter*, 1987

Giulio Paolini, *House of Lucretius*, 1981–84

Jannis Kounellis *Born* 1936 Piraeus, Greece

Holzer, Jenny
Ceiling Snake, 1996

This staircase connects the old section of Hamburg's Kunsthalle with a new building for contemporary art, and this fact became the starting point for Holzer's installation. Its centrepiece is an LED (light-emitting diode) screen almost 50 m (164 ft) in length, along which a never-ending sequence of messages flows. Mostly they move from the area of the old to that of the new, just as learning and artistic influences do. Around 1,000 messages in all run in a continuous loop some three hours long. All are uncontroversial: 'truisms', Holzer calls them. Some are in English, others in German; all are arranged in alphabetical order, specifically to exclude any sense of editorial manipulation or hierarchy of meaning. Although Holzer tends to work in text, she has never regarded herself as a writer. It is not her intention that her words in themselves should move or astonish.

Holzer does have deeper preoccupations, involving feminism, sex, death and war, but she does not set out to deal with these directly. Rather she hopes to draw attention to the way we are surrounded by media messages of every sort and the influence that these may have upon our thinking.

CREATED

Hamburg

MEDIUM

Mixed media

PERIOD/SERIES/MOVEMENT

Conceptual Art/Postmodernism/Neo-Pop

SIMILAR WORKS

Hans Haacke, *We Believe in the Power of the Creative Imagination*, 1980

Jenny Holzer *Born* 1950 Gallipolis, OH, USA

Gormley, Antony

Maquette for Leeds Brick Man, 1986

Courtesy of Leeds Museums and Galleries (City Art Gallery), UK/www.bridgeman.co.uk/© Anthony Gormley

This man-sized maquette (a three-dimensional model) is all that was ever made of the 'Leeds Brick Man', a figure intended to be 35 m (115 ft) tall. It was to stand on a patch of urban wasteland and help regenerate an area that had suffered severe economic decline. Antony Gormley's career has highlighted both the possibilities and the pitfalls of 'Site Works' (creations designed not as portable exhibits but as permanent fixtures for specific sites). His *Angel of the North* (1998) was really to capture the public imagination and give the mining town of Gateshead a new lease of life.

In the 1980s, though, that precedent did not yet exist and plans foundered in the face of vociferous opposition. For some the Brick Man was the Tate Bricks all over again: it was seen simply as a waste of public money. Others liked the idea of celebrating their city's industrial past, but objected that Leeds had never been a brick-making centre. Some feminists felt it inappropriate that a male figure should loom so large over a region so recently terrorized by the vicious sex-attacker Peter Sutcliffe, the 'Yorkshire Ripper'.

CREATED

England

MEDIUM

Brick

PERIOD/SERIES/MOVEMENT

Site Works

SIMILAR WORKS

Claes Oldenburg and Cloosje van Bruggen, *Batcolumn*, 1977

Christo and Jeanne-Claude, *The Gates*, 2005

Antony Gormley *Born* 1950 London, England

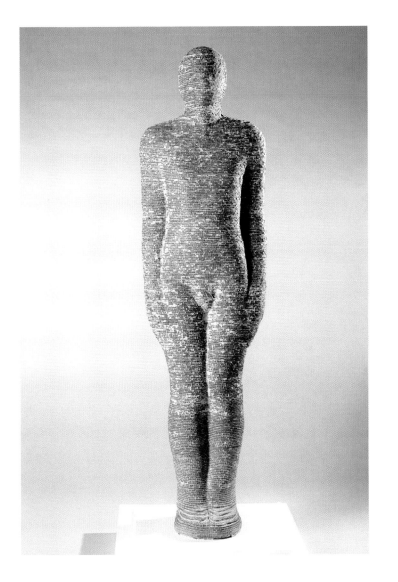

Bourgeois, Louise
Decontractée, 1990

In the field of sculpture, as in painting, the advent of Neo-Expressionism in the 1980s saw a second coming of artists from an earlier age. Louise Bourgeois is one example. Born in 1911 she had studied with Fernand Léger (1881–1955) in the 1930s and come to international prominence in the years following the Second World War. A veteran by the 1950s, by 1966 she was in a position to make what amounted to a 'comeback' when her works took center stage in a New York exhibition dedicated to 'Eccentric Abstraction'. The description suited her Surrealist-inflected imagination and still applied in the 1980s when Bourgeois was rediscovered and her works were re-presented through a Neo-Expressionist prism.

The contrast of delicate hands and massive masonry here is reminiscent of the work of Czech sculptor Miroslaw Balka (b. 1958). Although almost half a century younger than Bourgeois, he was brought up in a similarly traditionalist school that sets him apart from other Neo-Expressionists such as Julian Schnabel (b. 1951). Specifically he was trained in the creation of monumental stonework, a background he was able to exploit to ironic effect in a work like *Dawn* (1955).

CREATED

New York

MEDIUM

Marble and steel

PERIOD/SERIES/MOVEMENT

Neo-Expressionism

SIMILAR WORKS

Julian Schnabel, *Galileo's Table*, 1985–89

Miroslaw Balka, *Dawn*, 1995

Louise Bourgeois *Born* 1911 Paris, France

Kapoor, Anish

En Busca de la Montana, 1984

There is a hint of the organic about this extravagant efflorescence, but here the similarity with Moore and Hepworth ends. Anish Kapoor has brought something new and fresh to British sculpture, something with real feeling and ebullient emotion, rather than an idea to be articulated, which is why he is generally grouped together with the painters of the Neo-Expressionist school. His works, he says, are 'signs of a state of being'.

So too are those of a number of other sculptors, many of them often seen as 'Conceptual Artists' – Britain's Rachel Whiteread (b. 1963), for example. *House* (1993), her cast of the interior of a house condemned for demolition in the East End of London, was undoubtedly impressive in its ingenuity, but it was most striking in the sense of absence, of melancholy, it expressed. A still more tragic mood is suggested by the Dresden-like ruins to be seen in some of the most powerful 'Architectural Sculpture' of Germany's Isa Genzken. The 'Abakans' of Poland's Magdalena Abakanowicz are astonishingly evocative groupings of stone figures and bring Neo-Expressionism into the outdoor realm of Earth Art.

CREATED

London

MEDIUM

Mixed media

PERIOD/SERIES/MOVEMENT

Neo-Expressionism/New British Sculpture

SIMILAR WORKS

Rachel Whiteread, *Untitled (Yellow Bath)*, 1996

Anish Kapoor *Born* 1954 Bombay, India

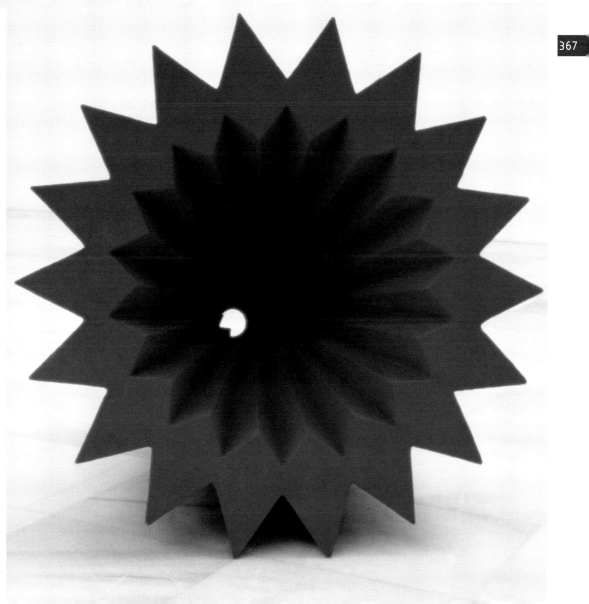

Koons, Jeff
Three Ball Total Equilibrium Tank, 1985

'Two Spalding Shaq Attaq, One Spalding NBA Tip-Off', adds a scrupulous subtitle to a work that reduces action to inventory; the thrills of sport to the stasis of the museum piece. The 1980s were arguably about ownership, money and possessions and Koons was the ultimate 1980s artist, having come to art from a career on Wall Street. Up there too with money as the mark of status is sex: life first imitated art as Koons married Italian porn-star Cicciona and then became a subject for it in some explicit images of the couple.

Koons also sensed the connection between unlimited affluence and kitsch, as can be seen in the spectacular 'puppy sculpture' in wood, steel earth and living flowers, which he created at Arolsen, Germany, in 1992. Something of the same joyous celebration of vulgar excess is to be seen in a painting like *Cake* (1985–87), a Superrealist-style representation of an extravagantly iced cake, with romantic rose, whose sheer pinkness practically sets the teeth on edge. More seriously it points to consumerism's creation of unrealizable yearnings: you can't have your cake and eat it, Koons implies.

CREATED

New York

MEDIUM & DIMENSIONS

Mixed media (glass tank, steel stand; three basketballs in solution of distilled water with sodium chloride reagent), 60$\frac{1}{2}$" × 48$\frac{3}{4}$" × 13$\frac{1}{4}$"

PERIOD/SERIES/MOVEMENT

Neo-Pop

SIMILAR WORKS

Haim Steinbach, *Pink Accent 2,* 1987

Damien Hirst, *Away from the Flock,* 1994

Jeff Koons *Born* 1955 York, PA, USA

Noland, Cady

Oozewald, 1989

'I'm interested in the differences and the similarities between blank identity and iconography,' says Cady Noland, 'as well as between anonymity and fame.' The mass culture celebrated by Pop Art apparently united the world, yet left individuals more isolated than ever before. Lee Harvey Oswald was an anti-icon, the ultimate loner, blamed for the death of the decade's iconic president, John F. Kennedy in 1963, before being shot himself – on official orders, the conspiracy theorists claimed.

Noland casts a disenchanted eye over the Pop scene of the 1960s: here we see the little guy being obliterated by the forces of the status quo. The image makes a political point – Noland is clearly unconvinced by the Camelot legend, but her main preoccupation is with the place of the individual man or woman in society. 'High' Pop Art was the product of a postwar period in which consumer choice was supposedly empowering everyone. However, Noland finds only a conformism that was finally coercive. Some day, Andy Warhol (1928–87) had said, everyone would be famous for 15 minutes: the reality was a culture that buried individuals alive.

CREATED

New York

MEDIUM

Screen print on aluminium; two pennants

PERIOD/SERIES/MOVEMENT

Neo-Pop

SIMILAR WORKS

Robert Gober, *Wedding Gown/Hanging Man–Sleeping Man/Cat Litter*, 1989–96

Gavin Turk, *Portrait of Something That I'll Never Really See*, 1997

Cady Noland *Born* 1956 Washington, DC, USA

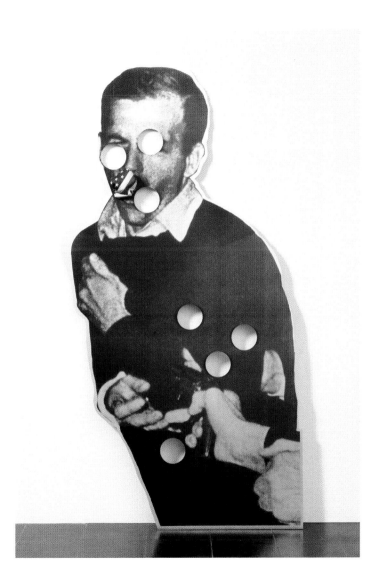

Perry, Grayson
Jar with Rude Words

Courtesy of Leeds Museums and Galleries (City Art Gallery), UK/www.bridgeman.co.uk/© Grayson Perry

London's Turner Prize has a tradition of 'shock winners', but 2003's victor Grayson Perry stands out even among that controversial company. His is a self-consciously deviant approach: many works feature his female alter ego, 'Claire'; all offend social and, still more, artistic proprieties. The codes governing gender are only the most obvious against which he transgresses: *Mother of All Battles* (1996) has 'Claire' posing in a pretty dress whose 'ethnic' embroidery turns out to represent military aircraft and other images of war, while she herself hefts an automatic rifle. Perry likes to work with embroidery not just because it is 'feminine', but also because it is not regarded as a 'real' artistic medium. Likewise, he works with clay because, he says, 'it is held in such low esteem in the artworld'. Its association with excrement also plainly appeals to his Rabelaisian side.

Here the shapely symmetry of the classic vase is mocked by the puerile slogans and incongruous images adorning it. Several contemporary artists have at least implicitly picked up Jannis Kounellis' critique of the idea of the artwork as exhibit. Is this vase beautiful, or just silly?

CREATED

London

MEDIUM

Ceramic

PERIOD/SERIES/MOVEMENT

Neo-Pop/Neo-Naturist

SIMILAR WORKS

Rosemarie Trockel, *Balaklava*, 1986

Maurizio Cattelan, *Frank and Jamie*, 2002

Grayson Perry *Born* 1960 Chelmsford, England

McCollum, Allan

Over 10,000 Individual Works (detail), 1987–88

Buyers of the Model T Ford, its manufacturer is said to have promised, could have any colour they wanted, so long as it was black. The great paradox of mass production was that it opened up choices for ordinary people, while at the same time imposing certain norms. With the advent of the mass media, such regimentation began to enter the realm of culture, occupying and ordering the individual mind.

For art, a discipline in which the creative ego had long been sanctified, the challenge posed by this development was alarming. It was not just the threat of censorship, although the cosy consensus that developed could be intolerant of different attitudes and ideas, but the feeling that individual thought was being undermined and individual creativity devalued. Cady Noland addresses that problem; so too does Sherrie Levine. Allan McCollom appears more ambivalent in his view. He takes mass-produced items in great quantities and presents them to the public as though they were unique, individually crafted masterpieces in the traditional manner. He clearly wonders whether art is necessarily devalued by the coming of mass-production: does the work have to be a holy relic?

CREATED

New York

MEDIUM

Plaster

PERIOD/SERIES/MOVEMENT

Neo-Pop

SIMILAR WORKS

Cady Noland, *Installation View*, 1989

Allan McCollum *Born* 1944 Los Angeles, USA

Opie, Julian
Cultural Baggage, 1984

Art approached the Millennium in a slightly nervous mood, with 'Futurism' lying a long way in the past. Not that its promises of road and air travel, great wars and super-weapons had failed to be fulfilled: humanity and the earth were still reeling from the impact. Having started the century full of confidence, inspired and emboldened by one revolution after another, artists had ended up wondering whether they themselves were not going to be swept away.

With the coming of photography, industrial production and ultimately computers, did any role remain for the individual artist? Ideas were changing too, such eternal values as 'beauty', 'truth' and 'meaning' now exploded by developments in linguistics and philosophy. The 'Postmodern' artist could look back with envy at Old Master Franz Hals or modern Mondrian, even at the ultimate 'tortured genius', Van Gogh. Whatever their problems, their certainties had been secure. And yet, along with apprehension, there was excitement and expectation: the end of certainty might set the artist free. The old 'cultural baggage' could be jettisoned or used just as a new generation of artists saw fit: a world of new possibilities awaited.

CREATED

London

MEDIUM

Oil paint on steel

PERIOD/SERIES/MOVEMENT

Neo-Pop/New British Sculpture

SIMILAR WORKS

Tony Cragg, *New Forms*, 1991–92

Thomas Demand, *Archive*, 1995

Julian Opie *Born* 1958 London, England

Author Biographies

Michael Kerrigan (author)

Michael Kerrigan has written widely on every aspect of history, but has taken a special interest in developments in art, literature and culture, contributing the entries on these areas to the Starfire *Illustrated Encyclopedia of World History* (2001). He has written several histories of various countries and civilizations, while his extensive work on literature includes the Shakespearean compilations *To Be or Not to Be: Shakespeare's Soliloquies* and *Shakespeare on* Love. His articles and reviews have appeared in the *Times Literary Supplement* and in the *Guardian* and *Scotsman* newspapers. He lives in Edinburgh.

Michael Robinson (foreword)

Michael Robinson is a freelance lecturer and writer on British Art and Design history. Originally an art dealer with his own provincial gallery in Sussex, he entered academic life by way of a career change, having gained a first class honours and Masters degree at Kingston University. He is currently working on his doctorate, a study of early modernist period British dealers. He continues to lecture on British and French art of the Modern period.

Picture Credits: Prelims and Introductory Matter

Further Reading

Ades, D., *Photomontage*, Thames & Hudson, 1976; revised edn 1986

Archer, M., *Art Since 1960*, Thames & Hudson, 1997

Brettell, R. R., *Modern Art: 1851–1929: Capitalism and Representation*, Oxford University Press, 1999

Bohm-Duchen, M., *Chagall*, Phaidon Press, 1998

Britt, D. (ed.), *Modern Art: Impressionism to Post-Modernism*, Thames & Hudson, 1974; new edn 1989

Carra, M., (tr. Tisdall, C.), *Metaphysical Art*, Thames & Hudson, 1971

Chilvers, I., *A Dictionary of Twentieth-Century Art*, Oxford University Press, 1998

Chipp, H. B., *Theories of Modern Art: A Source Book by Artists and Critics*, California University Press, 1968

Cork, R., *Annus Mirabilis? Art in the Year 2000*, Yale University Press, 2003

Cork, R., *New Spirit, New Sculpture, New Money: Art in the 1980s*, Yale University Press, 2003

Crook, J. & Learner, T., *The Impact of Modern Paints*, Tate Gallery Publishing, 2000

Dempsey, A., *Styles, Schools and Movements: An Encyclopaedic Guide to Modern Art*, Thames & Hudson, 2002

Dube, W-D., *The Expressionists*, Thames & Hudson, 1972; repr. 1996

Foster, H., Krauss, R. et al, *Art Since 1900: Modernism, Antimodernism and Postmodernism*, Thames & Hudson, 2005

Gayford, M. & Wright, K. (eds), *The Penguin Book of Art Writing*, Penguin, 1999

Harrison, C. & Wood, P. (eds), *Art in Theory, 1900–1990: An Anthology of Changing Ideas*, Blackwell, 1992

Hopkins, D., *After Modern Art, 1945–2000*, Oxford University Press, 2000

Hughes, R., *Nothing if Not Critical: Selected Essays on Art and Artists*, Harvill, 1990

Klee, F. (ed.), *The Diaries of Paul Klee, 1898–1918*, California University Press, 1964

Lucie-Smith, E., *Movements in Art Since 1945*, Thames & Hudson, 1969; new edn 2000

Meecham, P. & Sheldon, J., *Modern Art: A Critical Introduction*, Routledge, 2000

Rhodes, C., *Outsider Art: Spontaneous Alternatives*, Thames & Hudson, 2000

Richter, H., *Dada: Art and Anti-Art*, Thames & Hudson, 1964; new edn 1997

Riemschneider, B. & Grosenick, U. (eds), *Art at the Turn of the Millennium*, Taschen, 1999

Sandler, I., *A Sweeper-Up After Artists: A Memoir*, Thames & Hudson, 2004

Spalding, F., *British Art Since 1900*, Thames & Hudson, 1986; repr. 1992

Sylvester, D., *Interviews with American Artists*, Chatto & Windus, 2001

Tucker, W., *The Language of Sculpture*, Thames & Hudson, 1974

West, S., *Portraiture*, Oxford University Press, 2004

Index by Work

General Index